# CATCH A SUNFLAKE

## AUTHORS

ELAINE MEI AOKI
VIRGINIA A. ARNOLD
JAMES FLOOD
JAMES V. HOFFMAN
DIANE LAPP
MIRIAM MARTINEZ

ANNEMARIE SULLIVAN
 PALINCSAR
MICHAEL PRIESTLEY
NANCY ROSER
CARL B. SMITH

WILLIAM H. TEALE
JOSEFINA VILLAMIL
 TINAJERO
ARNOLD W. WEBB
PEGGY E. WILLIAMS
KAREN D. WOOD

**MACMILLAN/McGRAW-HILL SCHOOL PUBLISHING COMPANY**

**NEW YORK      CHICAGO      COLUMBUS**

# AUTHORS, CONSULTANTS, AND REVIEWERS

## WRITE IDEA! Authors

Elaine Mei Aoki, James Flood, James V. Hoffman, Diane Lapp, Ana Huerta Macias, Miriam Martinez, Ann McCallum, Michael Priestley, Nancy Roser, Carl B. Smith, William Strong, William H. Teale, Charles Temple, Josefina Villamil Tinajero, Arnold W. Webb, Peggy E. Williams

The approach to writing in Macmillan/McGraw-Hill Reading/Language Arts is based on the strategies and approaches to composition and conventions of language in Macmillan/McGraw-Hill's writing-centered language arts program, WRITE IDEA!

## Multicultural and Educational Consultants

Alma Flor Ada, Yvonne Beamer, Joyce Buckner, Helen Gillotte, Cheryl Hudson, Narcita Medina, Lorraine Monroe, James R. Murphy, Sylvia Peña, Joseph B. Rubin, Ramon Santiago, Cliff Trafzer, Hai Tran, Esther Lee Yao

## Literature Consultants

Ashley Bryan, Joan I. Glazer, Paul Janeczko, Margaret H. Lippert

## International Consultants

Edward B. Adams, Barbara Johnson, Raymond L. Marshall

## Music and Audio Consultants

John Farrell, Marilyn C. Davidson, Vincent Lawrence, Sarah Pirtle, Susan R. Snyder, Rick and Deborah Witkowski

## Teacher Reviewers

Terry Baker, Jane Bauer, James Bedi, Nora Bickel, Vernell Bowen, Donald Cason, Jean Chaney, Carolyn Clark, Alan Cox, Kathryn DesCarpentrie, Carol L. Ellis, Roberta Gale, Brenda Huffman, Erma Inscore, Sharon Kidwell, Elizabeth Love, Isabel Marcus, Elaine McCraney, Michelle Moraros, Earlene Parr, Dr. Richard Potts, Jeanette Pulliam, Michael Rubin, Henrietta Sakamaki, Kathleen Cultron Sanders, Belinda Snow, Dr. Jayne Steubing, Margaret Mary Sulentic, Barbara Tate, Seretta Vincent, Willard Waite, Barbara Wilson, Veronica York

# ACKNOWLEDGMENTS

*The publisher gratefully acknowledges permission to reprint the following copyrighted material:*

"Animal Fact/Animal Fable" is from ANIMAL FACT/ANIMAL FABLE by Seymour Simon, illustrated by Diane de Groat. Text copyright © 1979 by Seymour Simon. Illustrations copyright © 1979 by Diane de Groat. Reprinted by permission of Crown Publishers, Inc.

Jacket illustration from the Avon Books edition of BEEZUS AND RAMONA by Beverly Cleary, illustrated by Frederika Ribes. Text copyright © 1955 by Beverly Cleary. Reprinted by permission of William Morrow and Company, Inc.

From BICYCLE RIDER (Jacket Cover) by Mary Scioscia. Illustrations copyright © 1983 by Ed Young. Reprinted by permission of HarperCollins Publishers.

From BLACKBERRIES IN THE DARK (Jacket Cover) by Mavis Jukes with illustrations by Thomas B. Allen. Copyright © 1985 by Mavis Jukes. Illustrations © 1985 by Thomas B. Allen. Used by permission of Dell Books, a division of Bantam Doubleday Dell Publishing Group, Inc.

"Doctor De Soto" is from DOCTOR DE SOTO by William Steig. Copyright © 1982 by William Steig. Reprinted by permission of Farrar, Straus & Giroux, Inc.

"En un barrio de Los Angeles"/"In a Neighborhood in Los Angeles" from CUEPRO EN LLAMAS/ BODY IN FLAMES by Francisco X. Alarcón. Copyright © 1990 by Francisco X. Alarcón. Reprinted by permission of Chronicle Books.

Excerpt from "Free to Be . . . a Family" in FREE TO BE . . . A FAMILY by Mario Thomas & Friends. Copyright © 1987 by Free To Be Foundation, Inc. Used by permission of Bantam Books, a division of Bantam Doubleday Publishing Group, Inc.

From THE GIRL WHO LOVED THE WIND (Jacket Cover) by Jane Yolen. Illustrations copyright © 1972 by Ed Young. Reprinted by permission of HarperCollins Publishers.

"Grandfather Tang's Story" is from GRANDFATHER TANG'S STORY by Ann Tompert. Copyright © 1990 by Ann Tompert. Published by Crown Publishers, Inc. Reprinted by permission of the author and her agent, Kirchoff/Wohlberg, Inc.

From HANIMATIONS by Mario Mariotti. Originally published in Italy under the title RIMANI in 1989 by Fatatrac s.r.b. Florence, Italy. First American Edition 1989 by Kane Miller Book Publishers. Reprinted by permission of Kane Miller Book Publishers, P.O. Box 529, Brooklyn, N.Y. 11231.

From HENRY AND THE PAPER ROUTE (Jacket cover) by Beverly Cleary with illustrations by Louis Darling. Copyright © 1957 by Beverly Cleary. Used by permission of Dell Books, a division of Bantam Doubleday Dell Publishing Group, Inc.

"Houses" from UP THE WINDY HILL by Aileen Fisher. Copyright © 1953 by Aileen Fisher. Copyright © renewed 1981 by Aileen Fisher. Reprinted by permission of the author.

"How My Parents Learned to Eat" is from HOW MY PARENTS LEARNED TO EAT by Ina R. Friedman, illustrated by Allen Say. Text copyright © 1984 by Ina R. Friedman. Illustrations copyright © 1984 by Allen Say. Reprinted by permission of Houghton Mifflin Co.

"I Have a Friend" from NEAR THE WINDOW TREE by Karla Kuskin. Copyright © 1975 by Karla Kuskin. Reprinted by permission of HarperCollins Publishers.

Cover illustration from IN COAL COUNTRY by Judith Hendershot, illustrated by Thomas B. Allen. Illustration copyright © 1987 by Thomas B. Allen. Reprinted by permission of Alfred A. Knopf, Inc.

*(continued on page 327)*

Macmillan/McGraw-Hill School Division
10 Union Square East
New York, New York 10003

Printed in the United States of America
ISBN 0-02-178758-1 / 3, L.8
 3 4 5 6 7 8 9  VHJ  99 98 97 96 95 94 93

To Ramona and Tom Burt, Grandfather Tang and Tanya, Maurice and Shang, and all of the other characters and real people and animals who were put into this book especially for your enjoyment — Diane A. Altman

This book is also dedicated to all of the writers and artists; their words and illustrations make us think, laugh, and dream — Cynthia K. O'Brien

# What an Idea!

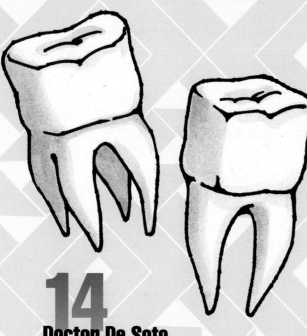

### *More to Explore*

### *Books from the Classroom Library*

### *Poetry*

A New View

## 172
### Science Magic

A science article
by Alison Alexander and Susie Bower

This assortment of science activities will have you making rainbows, seeing around corners, drawing motion pictures, and more!

# Family Ties

# CONTENTS

# WHAT AN Idea!

# Meet
# William Steig

What starts William Steig writing? Often it's a picture in his head! He once thought of a pig hanging from a string and began building a story that became *Roland the Minstrel Pig.* To continue a story, he says, "I just ramble around and discover for myself what will happen next."

Steig was sixty years old when he decided to create books for children. He thought of books he had liked as a boy, and he began writing and drawing pictures for that long-ago child. He was happy to discover that today's children enjoy his books, too.

Several of Steig's books have won awards. *Sylvester and the Magic Pebble* and *The Amazing Bone* won the Caldecott Medal, *Abel's Island* won the Newbery Medal, and *Doctor De Soto* was a Newbery Honor Book.

# Doctor De Soto

## by William Steig

**D**octor De Soto, the dentist, did very good work, so he had no end of patients. Those close to his own size—moles, chipmunks, et cetera—sat in the regular dentist's chair.

Larger animals sat on the floor, while Doctor De Soto stood on a ladder.

For extra-large animals, he had a special room.
There Doctor De Soto was hoisted up to the patient's
mouth by his assistant, who also happened to be
his wife.

Doctor De Soto was especially popular with the big animals. He was able to work inside their mouths, wearing rubbers to keep his feet dry; and his fingers were so delicate, and his drill so dainty, they could hardly feel any pain.

Being a mouse, he refused to treat animals dangerous to mice, and it said so on his sign. When the doorbell rang, he and his wife would look out the window. They wouldn't admit even the most timid-looking cat.

One day, when they looked out, they saw a well-dressed fox with a flannel bandage around his jaw.

"I cannot treat you, sir!" Doctor De Soto shouted. "Sir! Haven't you read my sign?"

"Please!" the fox wailed. "Have mercy, I'm suffering!" And he wept so bitterly it was pitiful to see.

"Just a moment," said Doctor De Soto. "That poor fox," he whispered to his wife. "What shall we do?"

"Let's risk it," said Mrs. De Soto. She pressed the buzzer and let the fox in.

He was up the stairs in a flash. "Bless your little hearts," he cried, falling to his knees. "I beg you, *do* something! My tooth is killing me."

"Sit on the floor, sir," said Doctor De Soto, "and remove the bandage, please."

Doctor De Soto climbed up the ladder and bravely entered the fox's mouth. "Ooo-wow!" he gasped. The fox had a rotten bicuspid and unusually bad breath.

"This tooth will have to come out," Doctor De Soto announced. "But we can make you a new one."

"Just stop the pain," whimpered the fox, wiping some tears away.

Despite his misery, he realized he had a tasty little morsel in his mouth, and his jaw began to quiver. "Keep open!" yelled Doctor De Soto. "Wide open!" yelled his wife.

"I'm giving you gas now," said Doctor De Soto. "You won't feel a thing when I yank that tooth."

Soon the fox was in dreamland. "M-m-m, yummy," he mumbled. "How I love them raw . . . with just a pinch of salt, and a . . . dry . . . white wine."

They could guess what he was dreaming about. Mrs. De Soto handed her husband a pole to keep the fox's mouth open.

Doctor De Soto fastened his extractor to the bad tooth. Then he and his wife began turning the winch. Finally, with a sucking sound, the tooth popped out and hung swaying in the air.

"I'm bleeding!" the fox yelped when he came to.

Doctor De Soto ran up the ladder and stuffed some gauze in the hole. "The worst is over," he said. "I'll have your new tooth ready tomorrow. Be here at eleven sharp."

The fox, still woozy, said goodbye and left. On his way home, he wondered if it would be shabby of him to eat the De Sotos when the job was done.

After office hours, Mrs. De Soto molded a tooth of pure gold and polished it. "Raw with salt, indeed," muttered Doctor De Soto. "How foolish to trust a fox!"

"He didn't know what he was saying," said Mrs. De Soto. "Why should he harm us? We're helping him."

"Because he's a fox!" said Doctor De Soto. "They're wicked, wicked creatures."

That night the De Sotos lay awake worrying. "Should we let him in tomorrow?" Mrs. De Soto wondered.

"Once I start a job," said the dentist firmly, "I finish it. My father was the same way."

"But we must do something to protect ourselves," said his wife. They talked and talked until they formed a plan. "I think it will work," said Doctor De Soto. A minute later he was snoring.

The next morning, promptly at eleven, a very cheerful fox turned up. He was feeling not a particle of pain.

When Doctor De Soto got into his mouth, he snapped it shut for a moment, then opened wide and laughed. "Just a joke!" he chortled.

"Be serious," said the dentist sharply. "We have work to do." His wife was lugging the heavy tooth up the ladder.

"Oh, I love it!" exclaimed the fox. "It's just beautiful."

Doctor De Soto set the gold tooth in its socket and hooked it up to the teeth on both sides.

The fox caressed the new tooth with his tongue. "My, it feels good," he thought. "I really shouldn't eat them. On the other hand, how can I resist?"

"We're not finished," said Doctor De Soto, holding up a large jug. "I have here a remarkable preparation developed only recently by my wife and me. With just one application, you can be rid of toothaches forever. How would you like to be the first one to receive this unique treatment?"

"I certainly would!" the fox declared. "I'd be honored." He hated any kind of personal pain.

"You will never have to see us again," said Doctor De Soto.

"*No one* will see you again," said the fox to himself. He had definitely made up his mind to eat them—with the help of his brand-new tooth.

Doctor De Soto stepped into the fox's mouth with a bucket of secret formula and proceeded to paint each tooth. He hummed as he worked. Mrs. De Soto stood by on the ladder, pointing out spots he had missed. The fox looked very happy.

When the dentist was done, he stepped out. "Now close your jaws tight," he said, "and keep them closed for a full minute." The fox did as he was told. Then he tried to open his mouth—but his teeth were stuck together!

"Ah, excuse me, I should have mentioned," said Doctor De Soto, "you won't be able to open your mouth for a day or two. The secret formula must first permeate the dentine. But don't worry. No pain ever again!"

The fox was stunned. He stared at Doctor De Soto, then at his wife. They smiled, and waited. All he could do was say, "Frank oo berry mush" through his clenched teeth, and get up and leave. He tried to do so with dignity.

Then he stumbled down the stairs in a daze.

Doctor De Soto and his assistant had outfoxed the fox. They kissed each other and took the rest of the day off.

Once, long ago, there was a woman who lived alone in the country with her three children, Shang, Tao, and Paotze. On the day of their grandmother's birthday, the good mother set off to see her, leaving the three children at home.

Before she left, she said, "Be good while I am away, my heart-loving children; I will not return tonight. Remember to close the door tight at sunset and latch it well."

But an old wolf lived nearby and saw the good mother leave. At dusk, disguised as an old woman, he came up to the house of the children and knocked on the door twice: bang, bang.

Shang, who was the eldest, said through the latched door, "Who is it?"

"My little jewels," said the wolf, "this is your grand-mother, your Po Po."

"Po Po!" Shang said. "Our mother has gone to visit you!"

The wolf acted surprised. "To visit me? I have not met her along the way. She must have taken a different route."

"Po Po!" Shang said. "How is it that you come so late?"

The wolf answered, "The journey is long, my children, and the day is short."

Shang listened through the door. "Po Po," she said, "why is your voice so low?"

"Your grandmother has caught a cold, good children, and it is dark and windy out here. Quickly open up, and let your Po Po come in," the cunning wolf said.

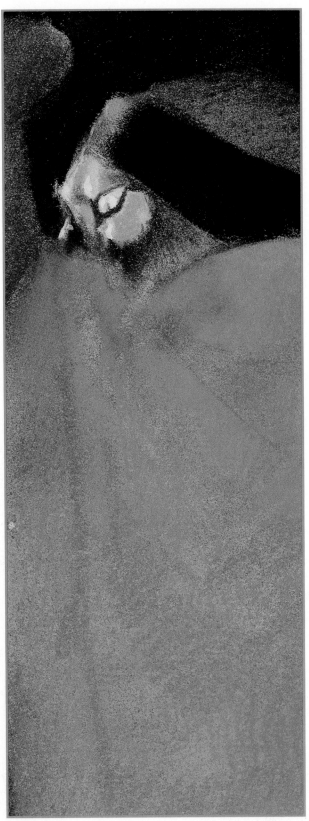

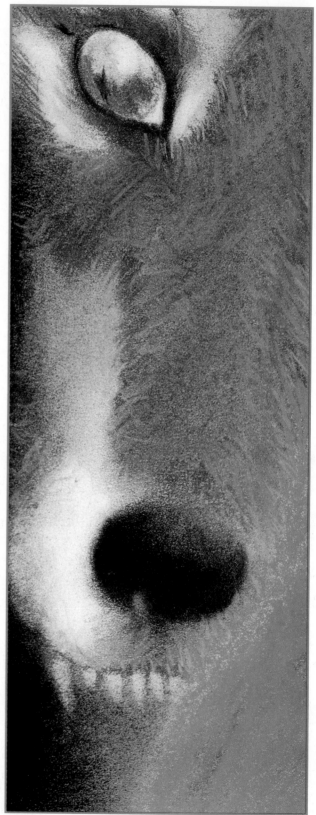

Tao and Paotze could not wait. One unlatched the door and the other opened it. They shouted, "Po Po, Po Po, come in!"

At the moment he entered the door, the wolf blew out the candle.

"Po Po," Shang asked, "why did you blow out the candle? The room is now dark."

The wolf did not answer.

Tao and Paotze rushed to their Po Po and wished to be hugged. The old wolf held Tao. "Good child, you are so plump." He embraced Paotze. "Good child, you have grown to be so sweet."

Soon the old wolf pretended to be sleepy. He yawned. "All the chicks are in the coop," he said. "Po Po is sleepy too."

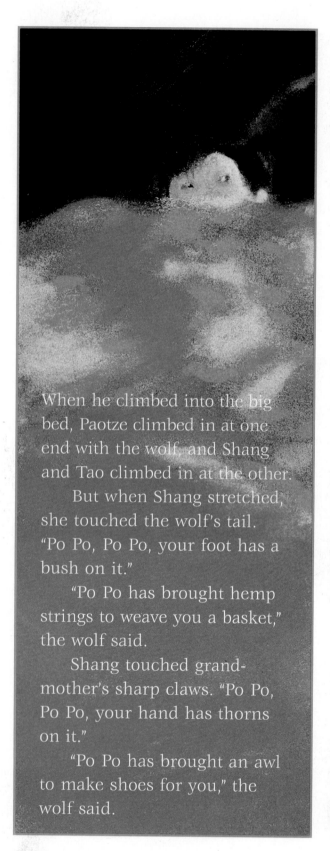

When he climbed into the big bed, Paotze climbed in at one end with the wolf, and Shang and Tao climbed in at the other.

But when Shang stretched, she touched the wolf's tail. "Po Po, Po Po, your foot has a bush on it."

"Po Po has brought hemp strings to weave you a basket," the wolf said.

Shang touched grand-mother's sharp claws. "Po Po, Po Po, your hand has thorns on it."

"Po Po has brought an awl to make shoes for you," the wolf said.

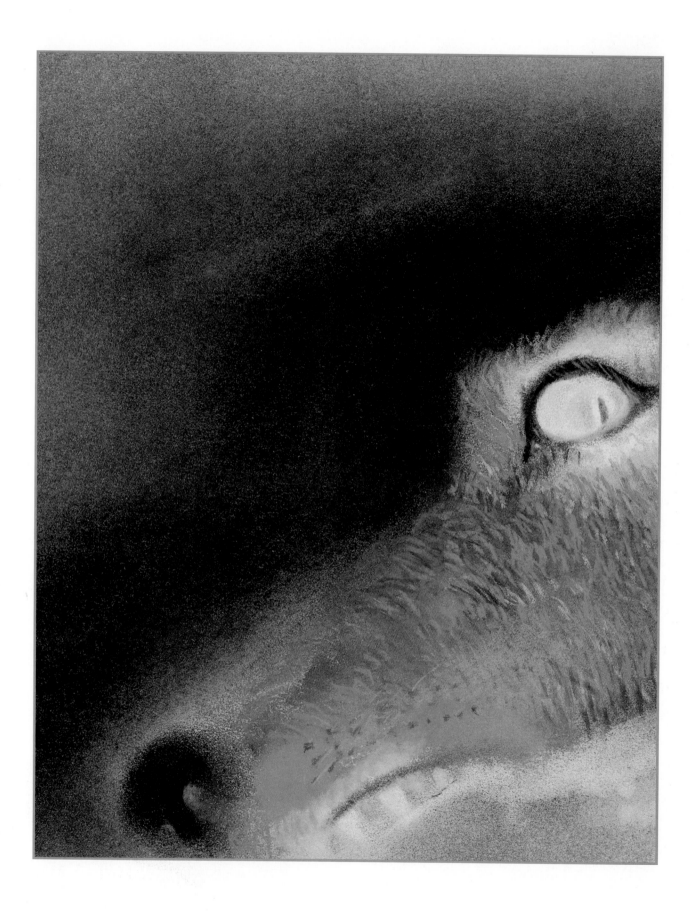

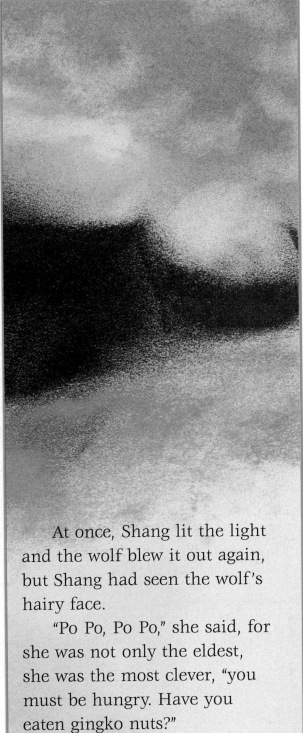

At once, Shang lit the light and the wolf blew it out again, but Shang had seen the wolf's hairy face.

"Po Po, Po Po," she said, for she was not only the eldest, she was the most clever, "you must be hungry. Have you eaten gingko nuts?"

"What is gingko?" the wolf asked.

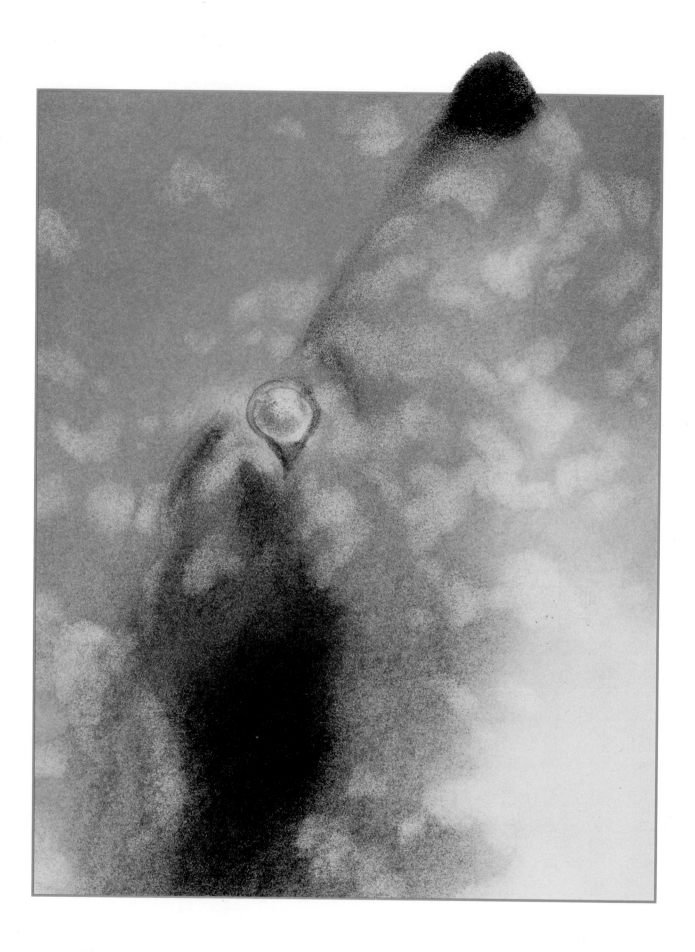

"Gingko is soft and tender, like the skin of a baby. One taste and you will live forever," Shang said, "and the nuts grow on the top of the tree just outside the door."

The wolf gave a sigh. "Oh, dear. Po Po is old, her bones have become brittle. No longer can she climb trees."

"Good Po Po, we can pick some for you," Shang said.

The wolf was delighted.

Shang jumped out of bed and Tao and Paotze came with her to the gingko tree. There, Shang told her sisters about the wolf and all three climbed up the tall tree.

The wolf waited and waited. Plump Tao did not come back. Sweet Paotze did not come back. Shang did not come back, and no one brought any nuts from the gingko tree. At last the wolf shouted, "Where are you, children?"

"Po Po," Shang called out, "we are on the top of the tree eating gingko nuts."

44

"Good children," the wolf begged, "pluck some for me."

"But Po Po, gingko is magic only when it is plucked directly from the tree. You must come and pluck it from the tree yourself."

The wolf came outside and paced back and forth under the tree where he heard the three children eating the gingko nuts at the top. "Oh, Po Po, these nuts are so tasty! The skin so tender," Shang said. The wolf's mouth began to water for a taste.

Finally, Shang, the eldest and most clever child, said, "Po Po, Po Po, I have a plan. At the door there is a big basket. Behind it is a rope. Tie the rope to the basket, sit in the basket and throw the other end to me. I can pull you up."

The wolf was overjoyed and fetched the basket and the rope, then threw one end of the rope to the top of the tree. Shang caught the rope and began to pull the basket up and up.

Halfway she let go of the rope, and the basket and the wolf fell to the ground.

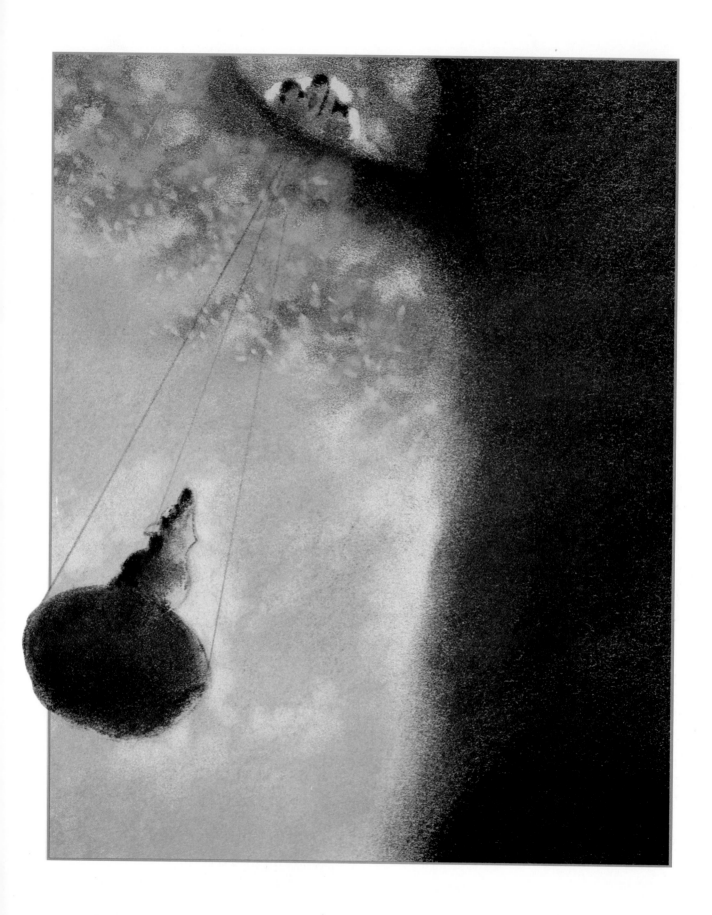

"I am so small and weak, Po Po," Shang pretended. "I could not hold the rope alone."

"This time I will help," Tao said. "Let us do it again."

The wolf had only one thought in his mind: to taste a gingko nut. He climbed into the basket again. Now Shang and Tao pulled the rope on the basket together, higher and higher.

Again, they let go, and again the wolf tumbled down, down, and bumped his head.

The wolf was furious. He growled and cursed. "We could not hold the rope, Po Po," Shang said, "but only one gingko nut and you will be well again."

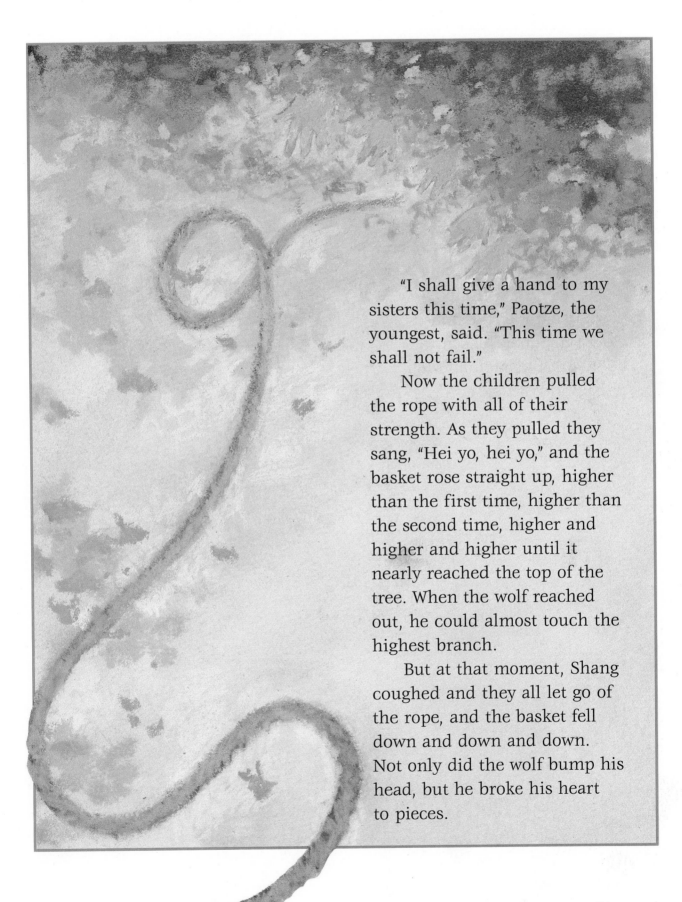

"I shall give a hand to my sisters this time," Paotze, the youngest, said. "This time we shall not fail."

Now the children pulled the rope with all of their strength. As they pulled they sang, "Hei yo, hei yo," and the basket rose straight up, higher than the first time, higher than the second time, higher and higher and higher until it nearly reached the top of the tree. When the wolf reached out, he could almost touch the highest branch.

But at that moment, Shang coughed and they all let go of the rope, and the basket fell down and down and down. Not only did the wolf bump his head, but he broke his heart to pieces.

"Po Po," Shang shouted, but there was no answer.

"Po Po," Tao shouted, but there was no answer.

"Po Po," Paotze shouted. There was still no answer. The children climbed to the branches just above the wolf and saw that he was truly dead. Then they climbed down, went into the house, closed the door, locked the door with the latch and fell peacefully asleep.

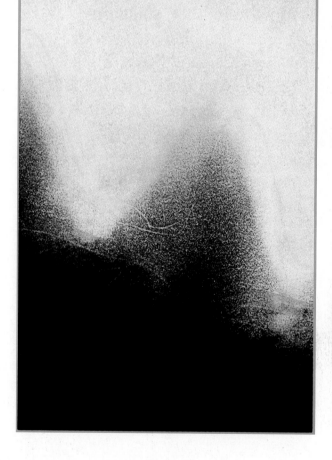

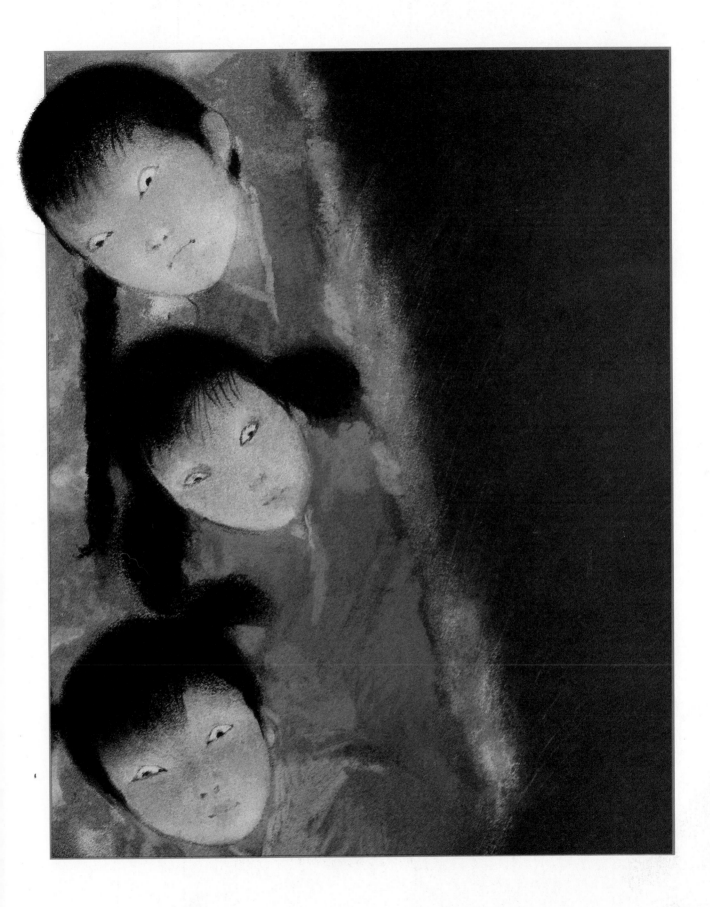

On the next day, their mother returned with baskets of food from their real Po Po, and the three sisters told her the story of the Po Po who had come.

MEET

Ed Young

While growing up in China, Ed Young loved to hear old Chinese folk tales. One favorite was the tale of Lon Po Po. As he listened, he never imagined that someday he would write the tale in English, add his own drawings, and win the Caldecott Medal.

Young remembers that he nearly always had a pencil in his hand when he was a boy. "I drew everything that happened to cross my mind: airplanes, people, a tall ship that my father was very proud of, a hunter and a bird dog that came out of my head." He kept on drawing when he moved to New York City and got a job. During his lunch hours, he sat in Central Park Zoo and drew animals.

One day Young was told to see an editor at a large publishing company. He carried a shopping bag containing animal drawings. The editor liked his work and asked him to do the drawings for *The Mean Mouse and Other Mean Stories*.

Since then, Young has drawn pictures for over fifty books, five of which he wrote himself.

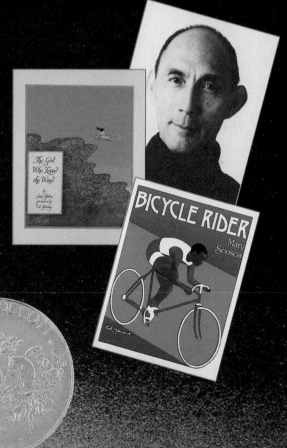

# The Inventor Thinks Up

# HELICOPTERS

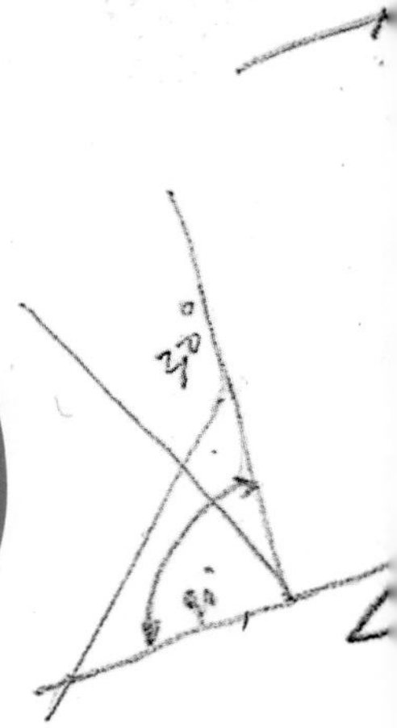

"Why not
a
vertical
whirling
winding
bug,
that hops like a cricket
crossing a rug,
that swerves like a dragonfly
testing his steering,
twisting and veering?
Fleet as a beetle.
Up
down
left
right,
jounce, bounce, day and night.
It could land in a pasture the size of a dot . . .
*Why not?"*

Patricia Hubbell

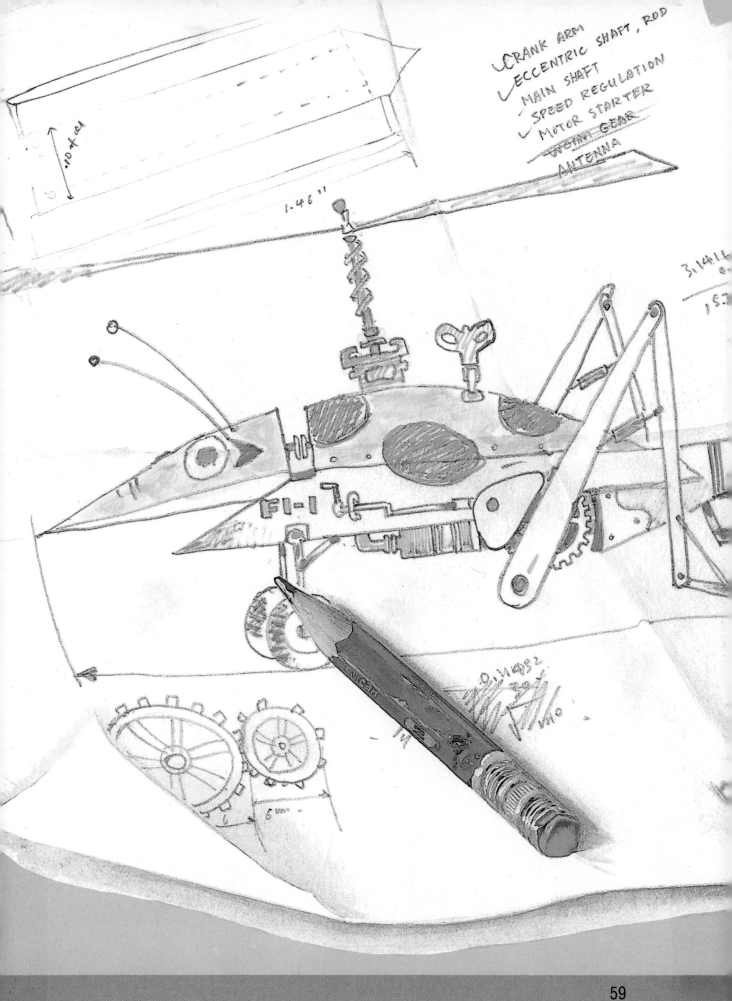

# ON WIND AND WING

**The Glorious Flight:
Across the Channel with
Louis Blériot**
by Alice and Martin Provensen,
Puffin Books, 1987

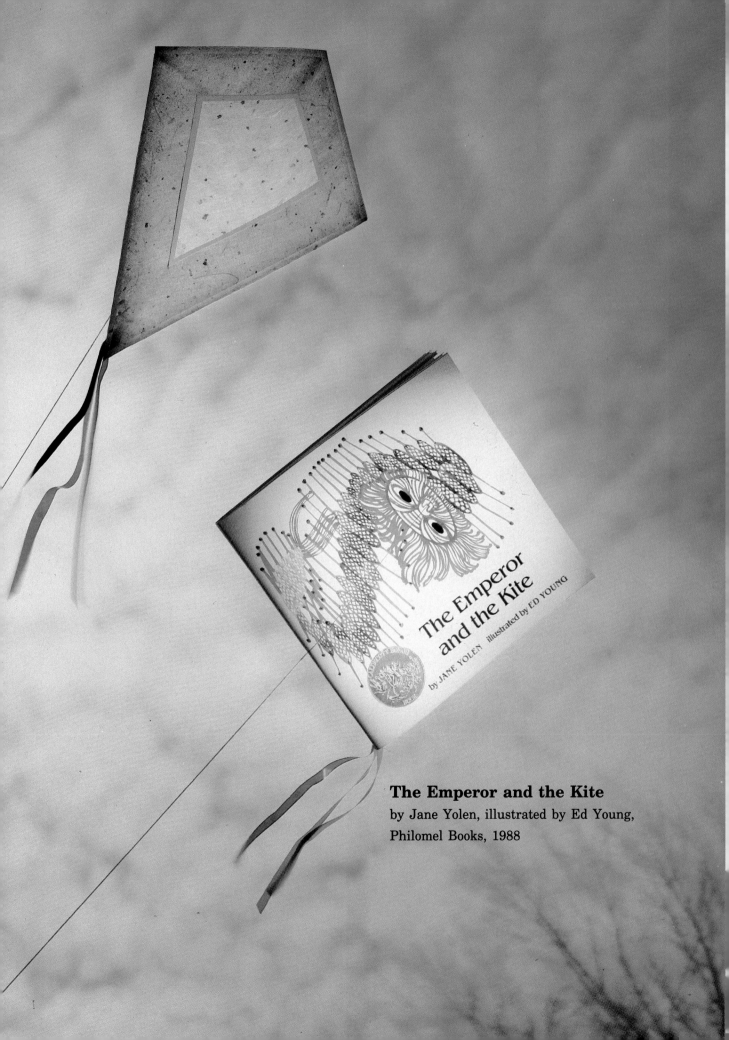

**The Emperor and the Kite**
by Jane Yolen, illustrated by Ed Young,
Philomel Books, 1988

# ANIMAL FACT/
# Animal Fable

## by Seymour Simon
## Illustrated by Diane de Groat

*W*e all know *facts* about animals—things that are true. But from watching animals and reading stories and tales about them, we may have some beliefs that are not true. We may believe in *fables* rather than facts.

In this science selection, decide whether each statement about an animal is a fact or a fable. Then turn the page to find out what scientists have discovered.

A turtle can walk out of its shell.

*Fable* When people find an empty turtle shell on the ground, they may think a turtle left it behind and moved into a new one. But that is not true. A turtle can no more walk out of its shell than you can walk away from your ribs.

A turtle's shell is not just a house it lives in. The shell is really part of the turtle's body. You should not try to take a turtle out of its shell. If you do, the turtle will die. The empty shells you may find on the ground are the remains of turtles that have died.

**Crickets tell the temperature with their chirps.**

**FACT** Crickets are animals whose body temperatures change with the temperature around them. On a hot day, crickets chirp so rapidly that it is hard to count the number of chirps. But on a cool day, crickets chirp much more slowly. We can then easily count the times they chirp.

Some people say they can use the number of chirps to find the exact temperature. That's not always possible. A cricket's chirping depends upon its age and health as well as on the temperature.

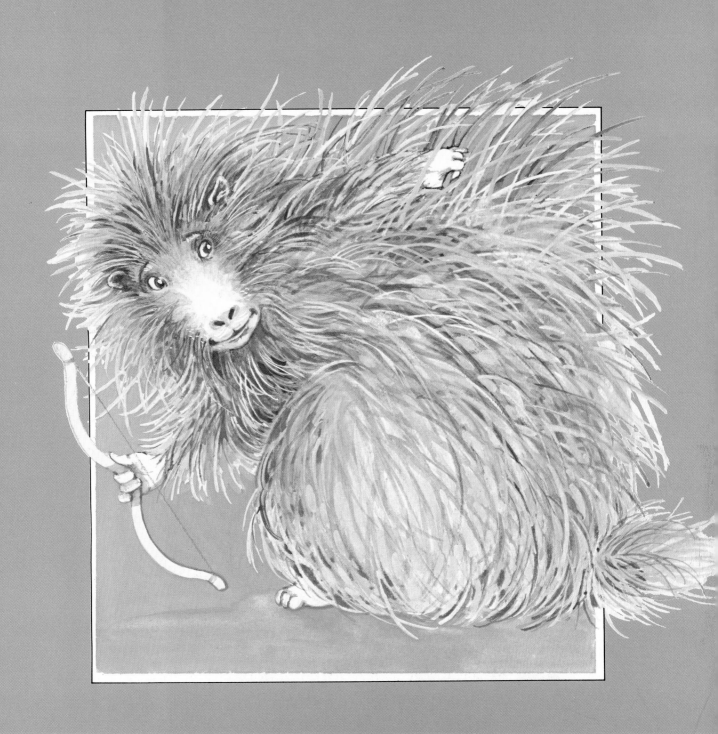

Porcupines shoot their quills.

*Fable* Porcupines cannot really shoot their quills. A porcupine's quills are sharp and have barbs like tiny hooks. The tip of a quill shown here has been magnified many times. When the quill sinks into an animal it becomes stuck and is left behind.

Porcupines use their quills to protect themselves. If an animal or person bothers a porcupine, the quills stand on end. The porcupine turns around and backs up to his enemy. Few animals bother a porcupine a second time.

**Dogs talk with their tails.**

# FACT

We know dogs don't use words to talk, but their tails can tell us how they feel. When a dog wags its tail from side to side, the dog is happy and playful. But when a dog wags its tail up and down, it may be because it has done something wrong and expects to be punished.

If a dog keeps its tail straight up, be careful. That is the signal that it may attack. Don't run, just back away slowly.

Ostriches hide their heads in the sand.

*Fable* There is a well-known fable that ostriches stick their heads in the sand when they are frightened. Here's how the fable may have started. When ostriches see an enemy, they sometimes drop down and stretch out their necks along the ground. This makes it more difficult for the enemy to see them. To a person watching an ostrich, it may look as if the ostrich has buried its head in the ground.

An ostrich may not be very smart, but it is not dumb. When an enemy comes close, the ostrich gets up from the ground and runs away.

**Goats will eat almost anything.**

**FACT** Goats will eat almost anything they can find. They even seem to eat tin cans. But they are not really eating the metal can; they are chewing the label to get at the glue underneath.

Though goats eat string and paper, they would rather eat fruit, vegetables, grass, and leaves of plants. They are not quite the "garbage cans" some people think they are.

# MEET
# SEYMOUR SIMON

Are you full of questions about the world? Do you wonder why fall weather turns some leaves red and others yellow? Is it a puzzle to you how a heavy ship can float? Science writer Seymour Simon likes questions like these. He says, "It's questions . . . that occur to me and that have been asked of me by children . . . that make me want to write science books."

Simon was a science teacher for twenty-three years. (He must have answered a million questions during those years!) Now he writes books full-time. Nearly 150 books with his name on the front are stacked on his shelves. More than fifty of them have received awards from the National Science Teachers Association. Among his award-winning books are *Mirror Magic, Stars,* and *The Moon.*

To answer questions for his books, Simon says he has "collected rocks, dug under rotting logs, tramped through swamps." He has also shared his home with earthworms, gerbils, ants, and crickets. He says about his books, "Sometimes I'll provide an answer, but more often I'll suggest an activity or an experiment that will let a child answer a question by trying it out."

# Thinking

Silently
Inside my head
Behind my eyes
A thought begins to grow and be
A part of me.
And then I think
I always knew
The thing I only got to know,
As though it always
Was right there
Inside my head
Behind my eyes
Where I keep things.

**Felice Holman**

# Mauric

## by Paula Fox

### illustrated by Doron Ben-Ami

Maurice's room measured six long steps in one direction and five in the other. The distance from the floor to the ceiling was three times higher than Maurice. There was one window through which Maurice could see several other windows as well as a piece of the sky. From the middle of the ceiling dangled a long string, the kind used to tie up packages of laundry. Attached to the end of the string was a dried octopus.

# Maurice's ROOM

It was the newest addition to Maurice's collection. When his mother or father walked into his room—which wasn't often—the octopus swung back and forth a little in the draught.

Maurice had used a ladder to climb up high enough to tack the string to the ceiling. The ladder was still leaning against the wall. Instead of returning it to Mr. Klenk, the janitor of his building, from whom he

81

had borrowed it, Maurice was using the steps for shelves. Even though Maurice's father, Mr. Henry, had put up a dozen shelves around the room for all of Maurice's things, there still weren't enough.

Maurice knew how to walk around his room without stepping on anything, and so did his friend Jacob. But no one else did.

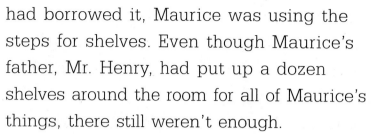

**A**s his mother and father often said to visitors, it was astonishing how much junk a person could find in one city block. His mother said Maurice kept their block clean because he brought up everything from the street to his room. His father said Maurice ought to get a salary

from the Department of Sanitation because of all the work he was doing in cleaning up the city. At least once a month Mr. and Mrs. Henry talked about moving to the country. It would be better for Maurice, they said. But then they would decide to wait a little longer.

Some visitors said that collections like Maurice's showed that a child would become a great scientist. Many great scientists had collected junk when they were eight years old. Other visitors said Maurice would outgrow his collection and become interested in other things, such as money or armies. Some suggested to the Henrys that they ought to buy Maurice a dog, or send him to music school so that his time might be spent more usefully.

In his room Maurice had a bottle full of dead beetles, a powdery drift of white moths in a cup without a handle, a squirrel hide tacked to a board, a snakeskin on a wire hanger, a raccoon tail, a glass of shrimp eggs, a plate of mealy worms, a box of turtle food.

There were things with which to make other things, such as nails of different sizes, screws, wire, butterfly bolts, scraps of wood, sockets, filaments from electric-light bulbs, cardboard from grocery boxes, two orange crates, a handsaw and a hammer. On the top of a chest of drawers Maurice kept stones and pebbles, dried tar balls, fragments of brick, pieces of colored bottle glass that had been worn smooth, and gray rocks that glistened with mica.

On his window sill there was a heap of dried moss next to a turtle bowl in which several salamanders lived half hidden by

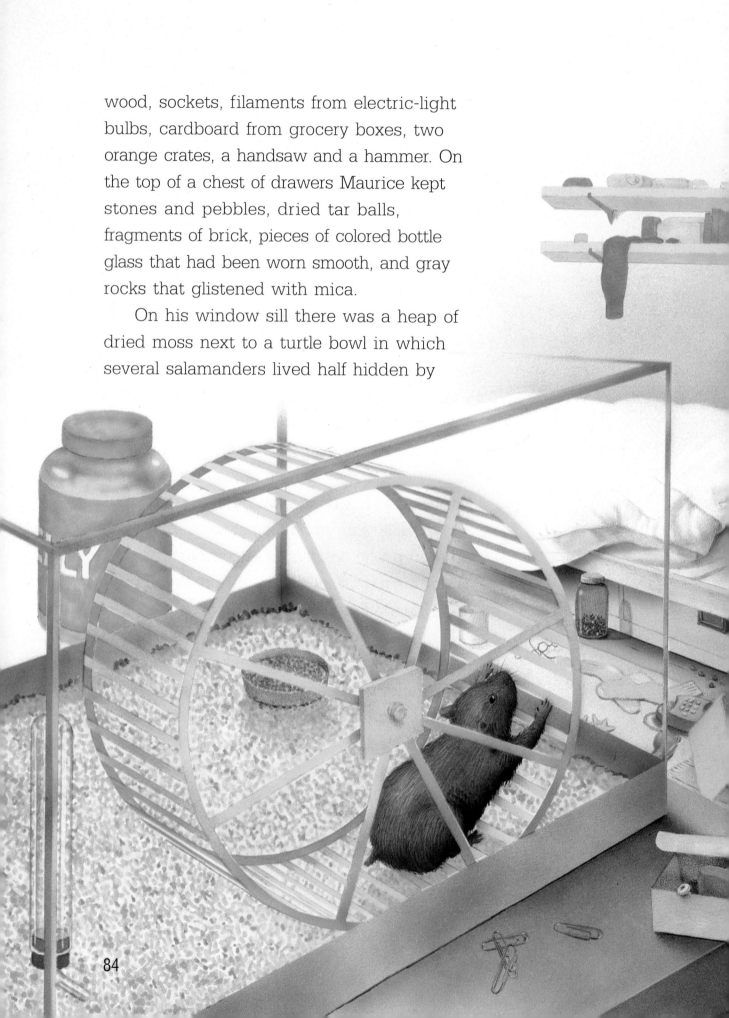

mud and wet grass. On the same sill he kept some plants from the five-and-ten-cent store. They looked dead. Now and then a cactus would put out a new shoot.

In another bowl on a table covered with yellow oilcloth were four painted turtles that were getting quite soft in the shell, and in a corner, in a square fish bowl with a chicken-wire roof, lived a garter snake and a lizard. An old hamster in his cage slept or filled his pouches with dried carrots or ran on his wheel. The wheel, which needed an oiling, screeched all night, the time the hamster preferred for exercise. But the noise didn't keep Maurice awake, only his parents. In a pickle jar, a garden spider sat in a forked twig, her egg sack just below her. Maurice also had a bird. It was a robin, blind in one eye and unable to find food for itself.

On the floor were coffee cans with things in them, an eggbeater with a missing gear, a pile of dead starfish, cigar boxes, clockworks, hinges, and a very large grater with sharp dents on all four of its sides. The grater was orange with rust, and it stood in the middle of the room beneath the octopus. You would have to use a magnifying glass to see all the other things Maurice had found.

His bed had two blankets and a pillow without a pillowcase. Sometimes a small goose feather pricked its way through the ticking, and Maurice would put it away in an envelope. He had used two pillowcases for his collecting expeditions, and after that his mother wouldn't give him any more.

There was one tidy corner in Maurice's room. It was where he had pushed his Christmas toys. They were a month old now, and the dust covered them evenly. They were like furniture or bathroom fixtures. Maurice felt there wasn't much to be done with them.

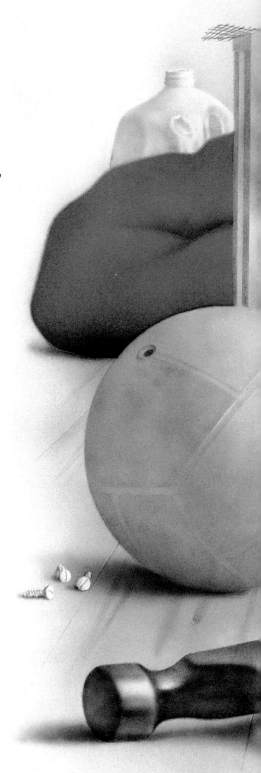

It was the end of January, and Maurice had just come home from school. He put his books on his bed and went to see what the snake was doing. It was lying on its rock. The lizard was watching it. The robin was so still it looked stuffed. But it cocked its head when Maurice whistled at it. The hamster was hiding bits of carrot in the sawdust at the bottom of its cage. The salamanders had buried themselves in the mud. Maurice was arranging little piles of food for his animals when he heard his uncle's voice from down the hall.

"Lily," his uncle was saying to his mother, "you ought to dynamite that room!"

"There must be another way," his mother said.

"You'd better give it up," said his uncle. "Maurice will never clean it."

"If we lived in the country, it would be different," said his mother.

"Perhaps," said his uncle.

87

Maurice took two walnuts from his pocket and cracked them together. His mother came to the door.

"Get everything off the floor," she said in a low, even voice as though she were counting moving freight cars.

"Where will I put things?" asked Maurice.

"I don't care," she said. "But clear the floor! Or else I'll bring in the broom, the dustpan, and a very large box. And that will be that!"

The doorbell rang. It was Jacob.

"Jacob can help you," his mother said.

Jacob was seven, but he looked bigger than Maurice. It was because he was wearing so many clothes—scarves, mittens, sweaters, two hats, and several pairs of socks. He began to take off his outer clothing, laying each item in a pile at his feet. Meanwhile Maurice explained the predicament.

"What are we going to do?" asked Jacob.

Maurice looked at the chest of drawers. The pebbles and rocks had been moved to the floor, and the chest was now covered with oatmeal boxes. He looked at the table. He could barely see the yellow oilcloth because it was hidden by sections of a witch doctor's mask he and Jacob had

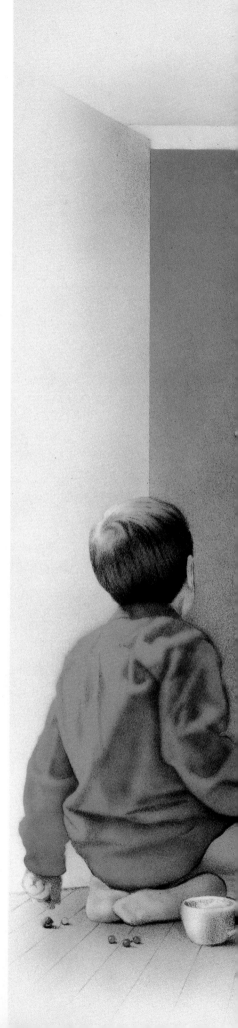

begun to make the week before. The turtles had been moved next to the salamanders on the window sill.

"There are five more floors in this room if you count the walls and ceiling," Maurice said to Jacob. Jacob looked smaller and thinner now that he was down to his shirt and pants.

"I see," said Jacob.

"We'll have to ask Mr. Klenk to help us," said Maurice.

Jacob began to sort out nails. Then he stopped. "But we won't be able to do that with everything! And how can we get it all done in just a day?"

"Mr. Klenk will know," said Maurice.

**M**r. Klenk, the janitor, lived in the basement five floors down. The basement smelled like wet mops, damp cement, pipes, and old furniture stuffing. But it was clean. Mr. Klenk had told Maurice that he couldn't relax a second or he would be drowned by the rubbish that poured out of all the apartments. "Overwhelming!" Mr. Klenk often exclaimed.

"It's a race between me and the junk," he would say. "If I let it get an edge on me, I'll get shoved right out of the city." But

Mr. Klenk didn't seem to feel the same way about Maurice's collection.

"Well, you're selective, my boy," he had said once, giving Maurice a caramel. "Besides, I suspect you've got something in mind for all that stuff of yours."

The two boys rang the janitor's bell. Mr. Klenk opened his door, blowing out a cloud of cigar smoke.

"I have to get everything off the floor," Maurice said. "Could you help us a little?"

"What do you have in mind?"

"There's plenty of space on the walls," said Maurice.

Mr. Klenk nodded and puffed on his cigar. "I know," he said. "But you didn't bring back my ladder, did you?"

"He forgot," said Jacob timidly. Mr. Klenk peered through the cigar smoke. Jacob backed away. The janitor in the building where Jacob lived sat in a big collapsed steamer trunk all day just waiting, Jacob was sure, for boys to wander by so he could pounce on them.

"Can you come now?" asked Maurice.

"Let's go," answered Mr. Klenk.

When they reached Maurice's room, Mr. Klenk stopped at the doorway.

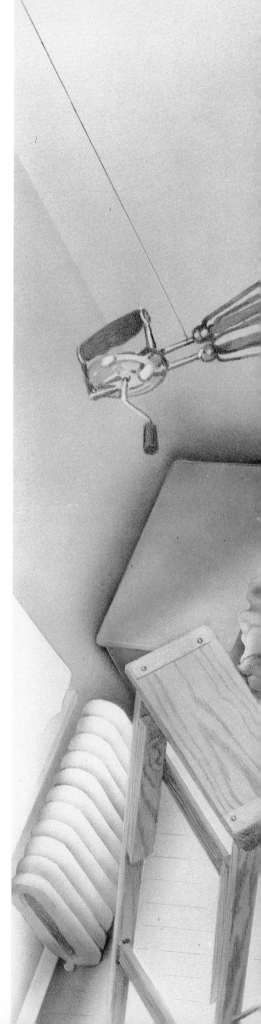

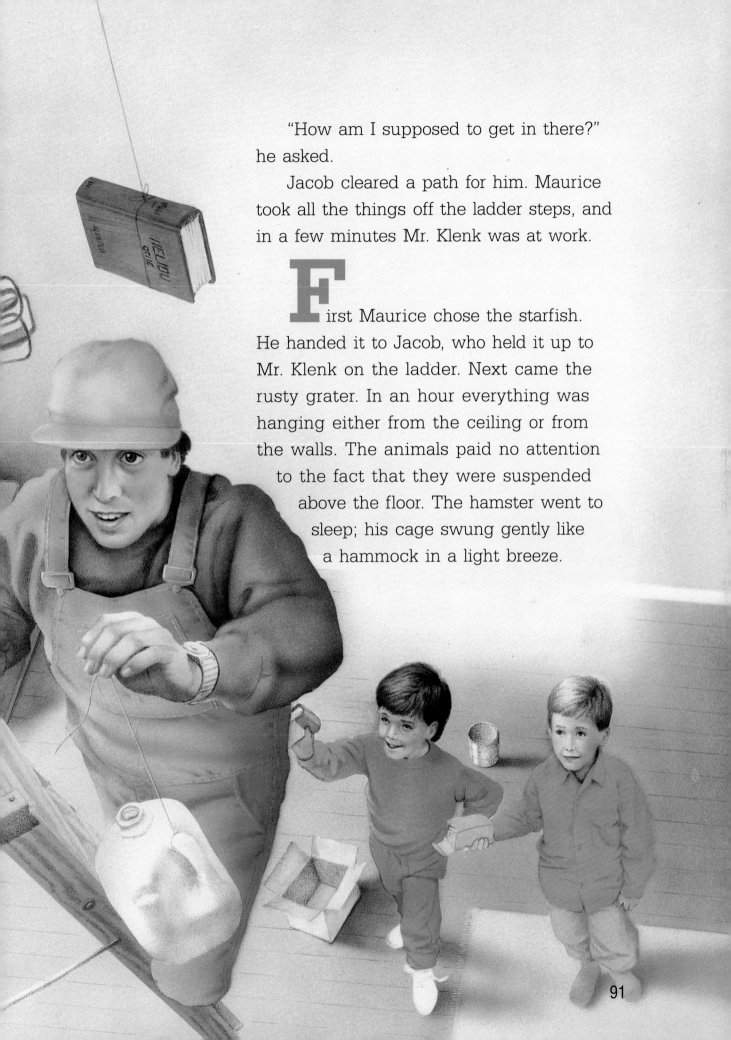

"How am I supposed to get in there?" he asked.

Jacob cleared a path for him. Maurice took all the things off the ladder steps, and in a few minutes Mr. Klenk was at work.

First Maurice chose the starfish. He handed it to Jacob, who held it up to Mr. Klenk on the ladder. Next came the rusty grater. In an hour everything was hanging either from the ceiling or from the walls. The animals paid no attention to the fact that they were suspended above the floor. The hamster went to sleep; his cage swung gently like a hammock in a light breeze.

By six o'clock, the floor boards appeared.
It was a good floor, and Maurice and Jacob
sat down on it.

"Now we have room for more things," said
Maurice.

Maurice's mother and his uncle came to
the door.

"Wow!" said Uncle.

Mrs. Henry looked pale. "I didn't have *that*
in mind," she said.

"Well, Lily, they've cleared the floor," said
the uncle.

## Meet Paula Fox

When Paula Fox saw the mess in her son's room, she complained, "Too many toys, too much junk." But then she noticed that the "junk" was actually quite interesting. With this in mind, Fox began *Maurice's Room*, her first book. She says, "I was off and running. The books just seemed to pour out of me."

Whenever Fox gets an idea, even if she is busy chopping onions, she writes it down in a notebook. The ideas in her notebooks have turned into more than twenty books, two of which have won the Newbery Medal. She feels that children deserve powerful, honest stories. "Children are not easily fooled," she says. "They know if a story is authentic or not."

# Nathaniel's

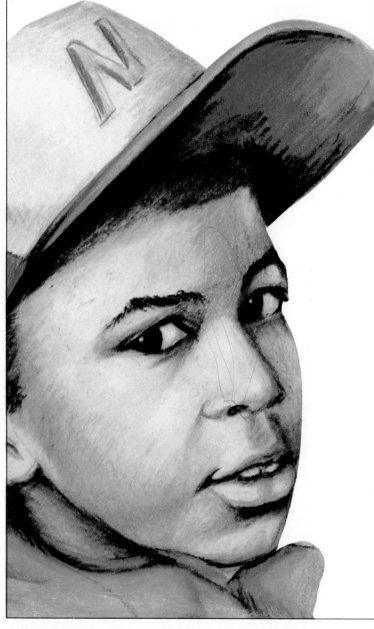

It's Nathaniel talking
and Nathaniel's me
I'm talking about
My philosophy
About the things I do
And the people I see
All told in the words
Of Nathaniel B. Free
That's me
And I can rap
I can rap
I can rap, rap, rap
Till your earflaps flap
I can talk that talk
Till you go for a walk
I can run it on down
Till you get out of town
I can rap

# Rap

I can rap
Rested, dressed and feeling fine
I've got something on my mind
Friends and kin and neighborhood
Listen now and listen good
Nathaniel's talking
Nathaniel B. Free
Talking about
My philosophy
Been thinking all day
I got a lot to say
Gotta run it on down
Nathaniel's way
Okay!
I gotta rap
Gotta rap
Gotta rap, rap, rap
Till your earflaps flap

Gotta talk that talk
Till you go for a walk
Gotta run it on down
Till you get out of town
Gotta rap
Gotta rap
Rested, dressed and feeling fine
I've got something on my mind
Friends and kin and neighborhood
Listen now and listen good
I'm gonna rap, hey!
Gonna rap, hey!
Gonna rap, hey!
I'm gonna rap!

**Eloise Greenfield**

95

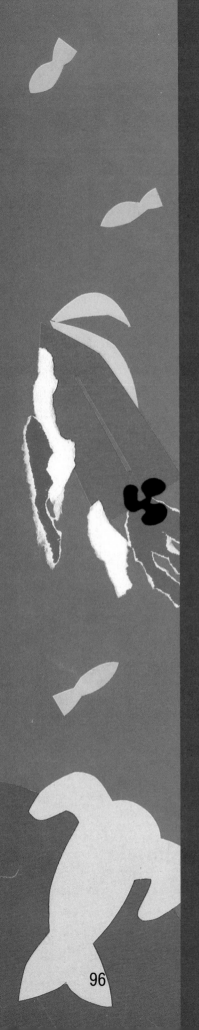

# CONTENTS

# A NEW VIEW

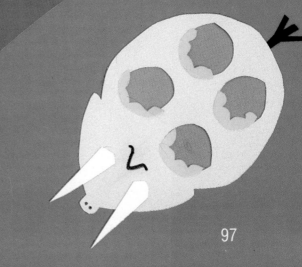

I have a friend who keeps on standing on her hands.
That's fine,
Except I find it very difficult to talk to her
Unless I stand on mine.

KARLA KUSKIN

98

# MEET *Chris Van Allsburg*

If you saw ants in your kitchen, what would you think? If you are like a lot of people, you might think "How disgusting!" or "How interesting!" or "How cute!" However, when Chris Van Allsburg saw two ants in his kitchen, he thought: "If I were an ant looking out from an electrical socket, the long slits in which the light poured in would look like 15-foot doorways hung in space." That thought gave Chris Van Allsburg the idea for *Two Bad Ants*.

Chris Van Allsburg's talent for looking at the world in unusual ways has won him the highest award for children's picture books in the United States—the Caldecott Medal. He won it not just once, but twice: for *Jumanji* in 1982 and for *The Polar Express* in 1986.

Van Allsburg's way of looking at the world has also won him many fans. One fan wrote: "I love the books you write. I am so glad you are weird because I am very weird. I think you are weird but great."

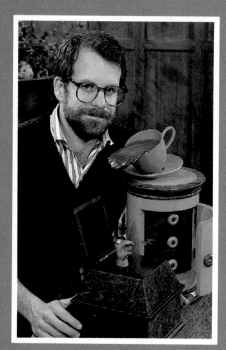

**Chris Van Allsburg, with some of the sculptures he has created**

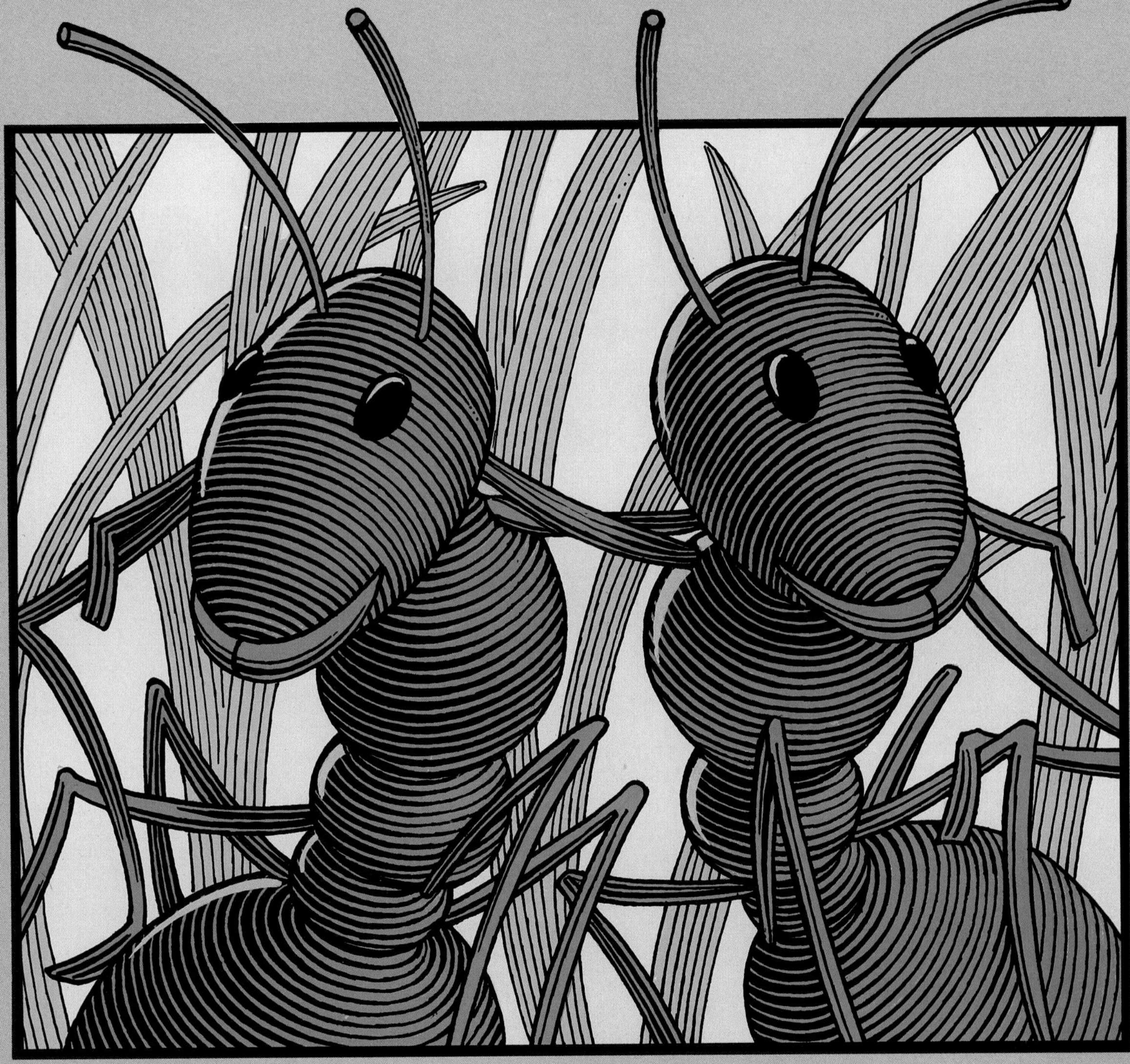

# TWO BAD ANTS

CHRIS VAN ALLSBURG

The news traveled swiftly through the tunnels
of the ant world. A scout had returned with a
remarkable discovery—a beautiful sparkling
crystal. When the scout presented the crystal to
the ant queen she took a small bite, then quickly
ate the entire thing.

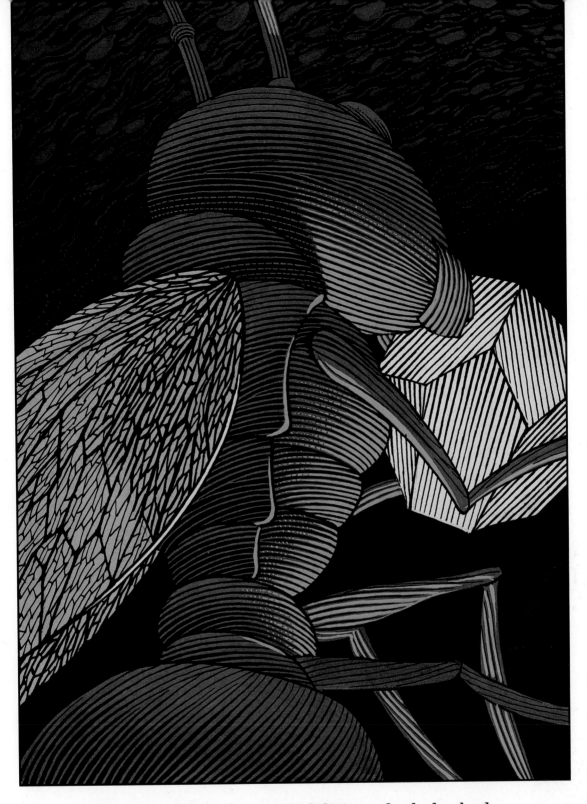

She deemed it the most delicious food she had
ever tasted. Nothing could make her happier than
to have more, much more. The ants understood.
They were eager to gather more crystals because
the queen was the mother of them all. Her
happiness made the whole ant nest a happy place.

It was late in the day when they departed.
Long shadows stretched over the entrance to the
ant kingdom. One by one the insects climbed out,
following the scout, who had made it clear—there
were many crystals where the first had been
found, but the journey was long and dangerous.

They marched into the woods that surrounded
their underground home. Dusk turned to twilight,
twilight to night. The path they followed twisted
and turned, every bend leading them deeper into
the dark forest.

More than once the line of ants stopped and anxiously listened for the sounds of hungry spiders. But all they heard was the call of crickets echoing through the woods like distant thunder.

Dew formed on the leaves above. Without warning, huge cold drops fell on the marching ants. A firefly passed overhead that, for an instant, lit up the woods with a blinding flash of blue-green light.

At the edge of the forest stood a mountain. The ants looked up and could not see its peak. It seemed to reach right to the heavens. But they did not stop. Up the side they climbed, higher and higher.

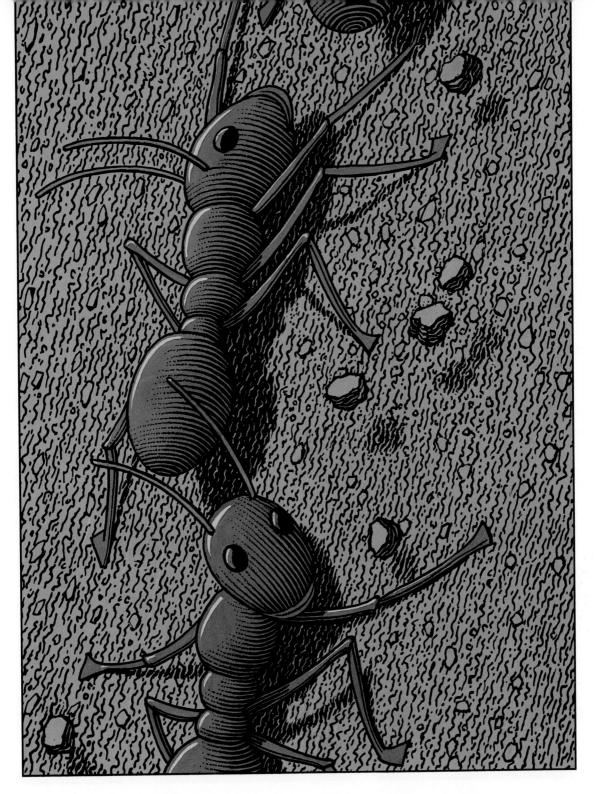

The wind whistled through the cracks of the
mountain's face. The ants could feel its force bending
their delicate antennae. Their legs grew weak as
they struggled upward. At last they reached a ledge
and crawled through a narrow tunnel.

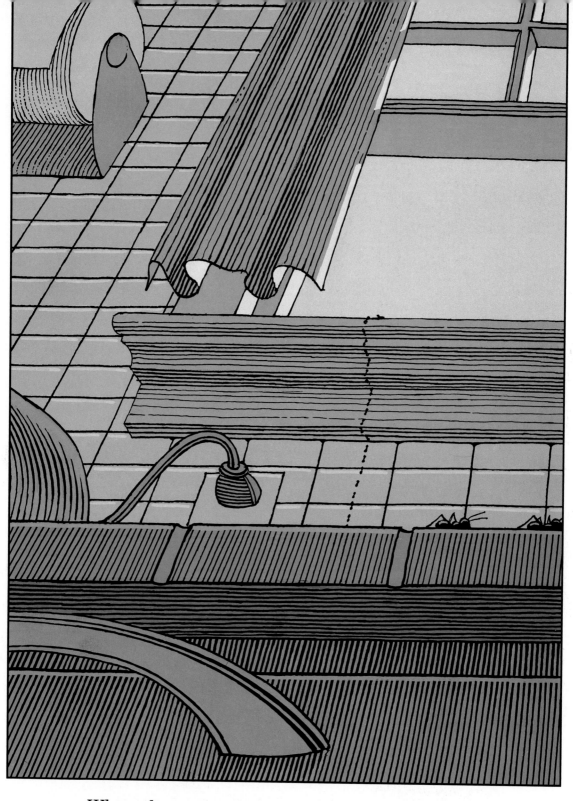

When the ants came out of the tunnel they
found themselves in a strange world. Smells they
had known all their lives, smells of dirt and grass
and rotting plants, had vanished. There was no
more wind and, most puzzling of all, it seemed
that the sky was gone.

They crossed smooth shiny surfaces, then
followed the scout up a glassy, curved wall. They
had reached their goal. From the top of the wall
they looked below to a sea of crystals. One by one
the ants climbed down into the sparkling treasure.

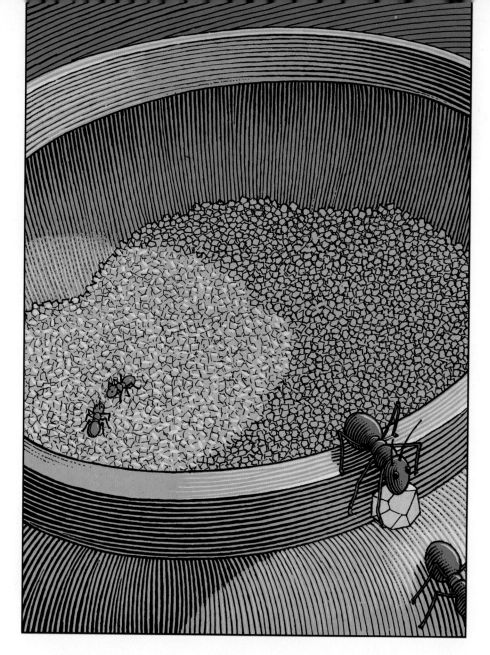

Quickly they each chose a crystal, then turned
to start the journey home. There was something
about this unnatural place that made the ants
nervous. In fact they left in such a hurry that
none of them noticed the two small ants who
stayed behind.

"Why go back?" one asked the other. "This
place may not feel like home, but look at all these
crystals." "You're right," said the other, "we can
stay here and eat this tasty treasure every day,
forever." So the two ants ate crystal after crystal
until they were too full to move, and fell asleep.

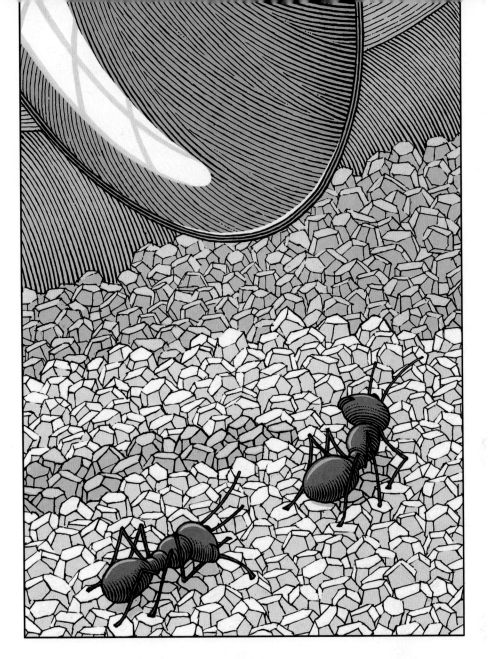

Daylight came. The sleeping ants were
unaware of changes taking place in their new
found home. A giant silver scoop hovered above
them, then plunged deep into the crystals. It
shoveled up both ants and crystals and carried
them high into the air.

The ants were wide awake when the scoop
turned, dropping them from a frightening height.
They tumbled through space in a shower of
crystals and fell into a boiling brown lake.

Then the giant scoop stirred violently back and forth. Crushing waves fell over the ants. They paddled hard to keep their tiny heads above water. But the scoop kept spinning the hot brown liquid.

Around and around it went, creating a whirlpool that sucked the ants deeper and deeper. They both held their breath and finally bobbed to the surface, gasping for air and spitting mouthfuls of the terrible, bitter water.

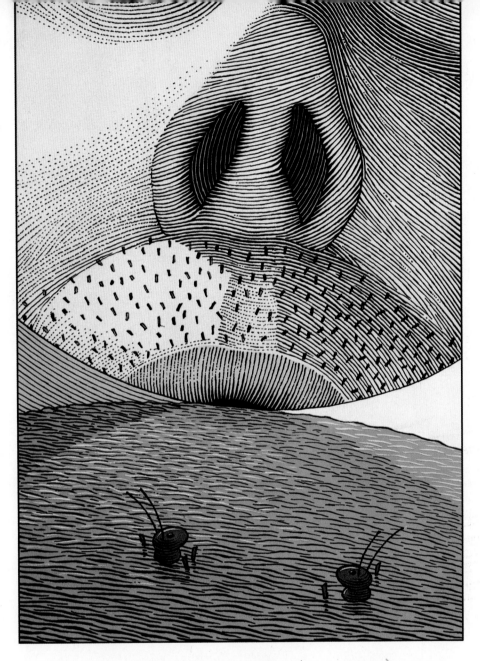

Then the lake tilted and began to empty into a cave. The ants could hear the rushing water and felt themselves pulled toward the pitch black hole. Suddenly the cave disappeared and the lake became calm. The ants swam to the shore and found that the lake had steep sides.

They hurried down the walls that held back the lake. The frightened insects looked for a place to hide, worried that the giant scoop might shovel them up again. Close by they found a huge round disk with holes that could neatly hide them.

But as soon as they had climbed inside, their
hiding place was lifted, tilted, and lowered into a
dark space. When the ants climbed out of the
holes they were surrounded by a strange red glow.
It seemed to them that every second the
temperature was rising.

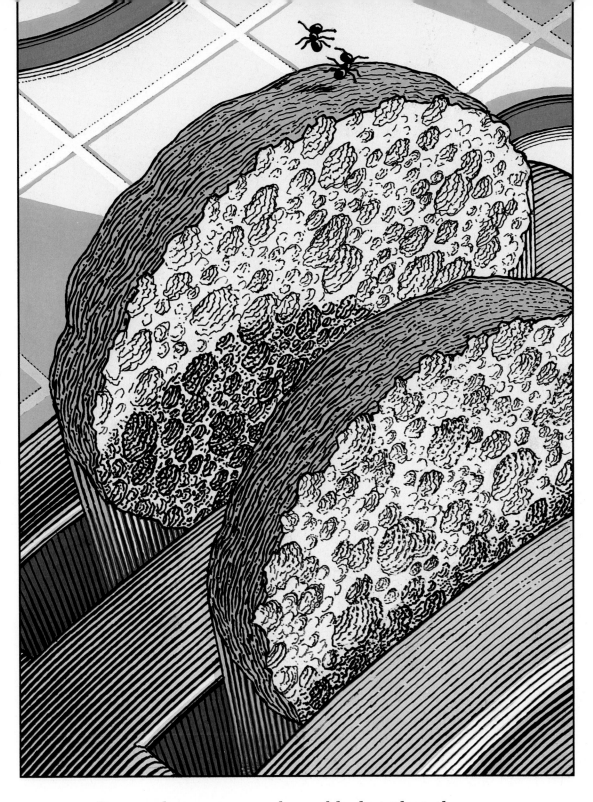

It soon became so unbearably hot that they thought they would soon be cooked. But suddenly the disk they were standing on rocketed upward and the two hot ants went flying through the air.

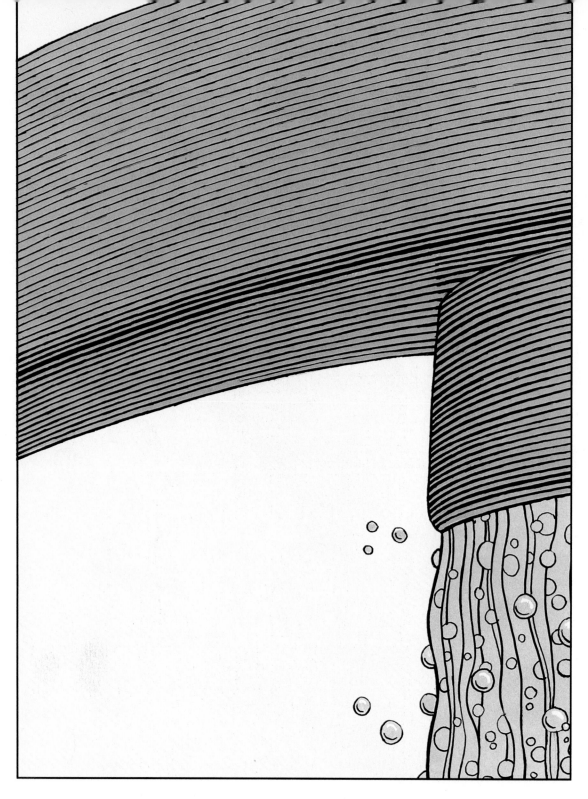

They landed near what seemed to be a
fountain—a waterfall pouring from a silver tube.
Both ants had a powerful thirst and longed to dip
their feverish heads into the refreshing water.
They quickly climbed along the tube.

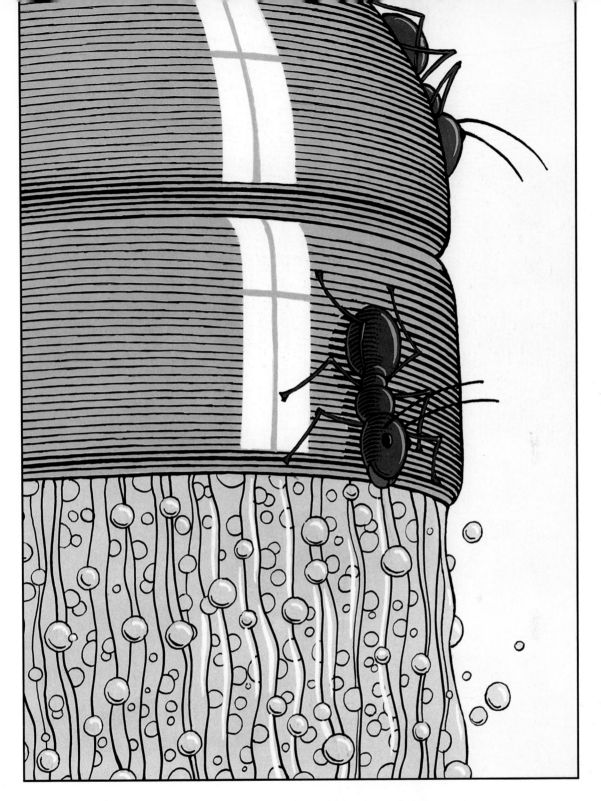

As they got closer to the rushing water the ants felt a cool spray. They tightly gripped the shiny surface of the fountain and slowly leaned their heads into the falling stream. But the force of the water was much too strong.

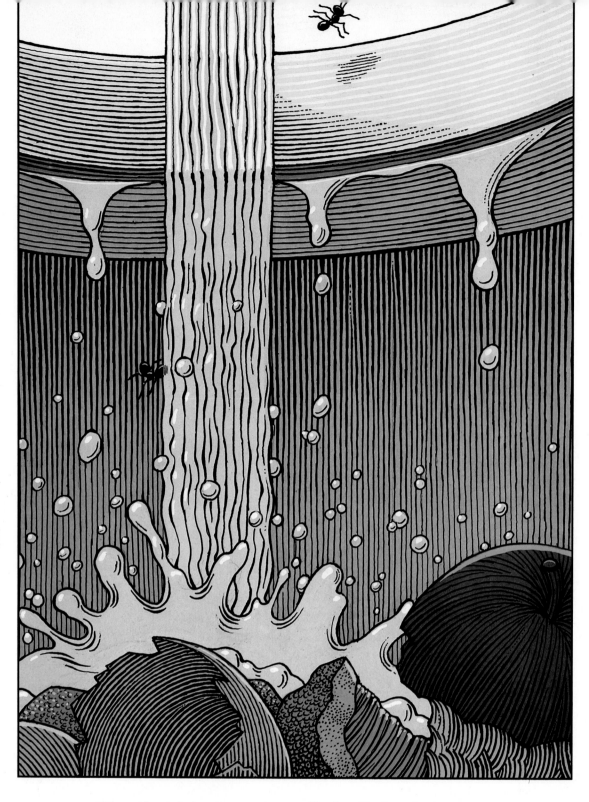

The tiny insects were pulled off the fountain
and plunged down into a wet, dark chamber. They
landed on half-eaten fruit and other soggy things.
Suddenly the air was filled with loud, frightening
sounds. The chamber began to spin.

The ants were caught in a whirling storm of shredded food and stinging rain. Then, just as quickly as it had started, the noise and spinning stopped. Bruised and dizzy, the ants climbed out of the chamber.

In daylight once again, they raced through
puddles and up a smooth metal wall. In the
distance they saw something comforting—two long,
narrow holes that reminded them of the warmth
and safety of their old underground home. They
climbed up into the dark openings.

But there was no safety inside these holes. A strange force passed through the wet ants. They were stunned senseless and blown out of the holes like bullets from a gun. When they landed the tiny insects were too exhausted to go on. They crawled into a dark corner and fell fast asleep.

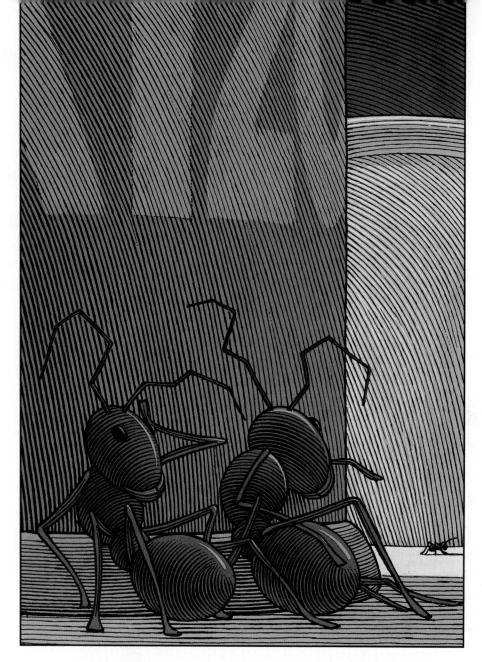

Night had returned when the battered ants awoke to a familiar sound—the footsteps of their fellow insects returning for more crystals. The two ants slipped quietly to the end of the line. They climbed the glassy wall and once again stood amid the treasure. But this time they each chose a single crystal and followed their friends home.

Standing at the edge of their ant hole, the
two ants listened to the joyful sounds that came
from below. They knew how grateful their
mother queen would be when they gave her
their crystals. At that moment, the two ants felt
happier than they'd ever felt before. This was
their home, this was their family. This was
where they were meant to be.

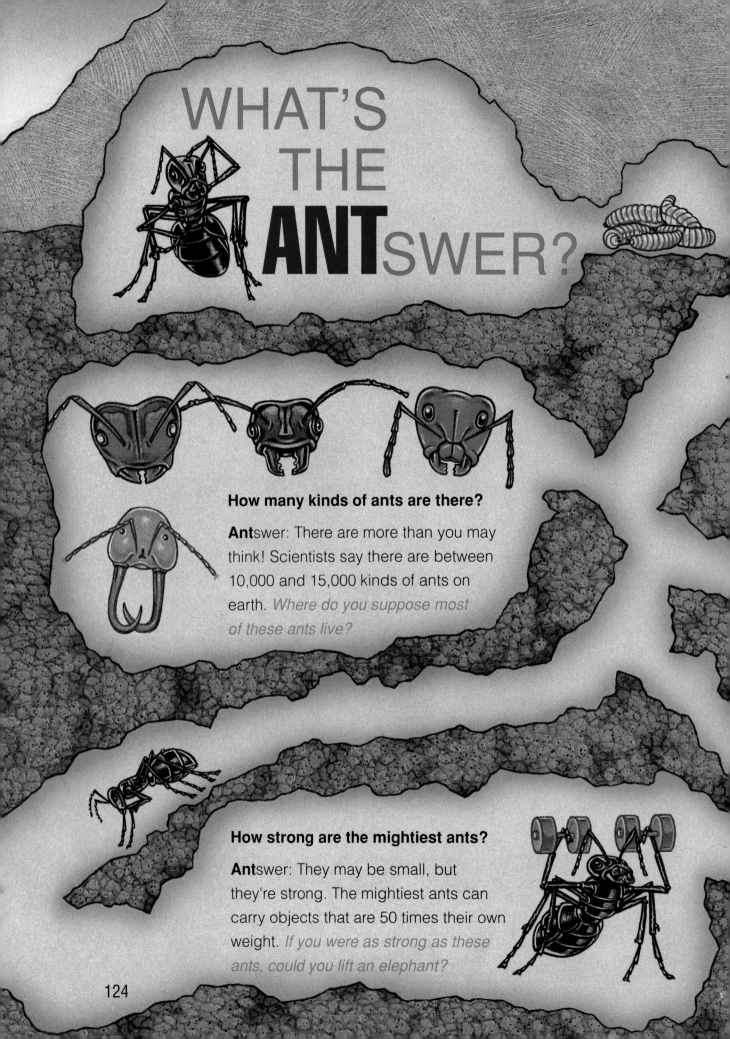

# WHAT'S THE **ANT**SWER?

### How many kinds of ants are there?

**Ant**swer: There are more than you may think! Scientists say there are between 10,000 and 15,000 kinds of ants on earth. *Where do you suppose most of these ants live?*

### How strong are the mightiest ants?

**Ant**swer: They may be small, but they're strong. The mightiest ants can carry objects that are 50 times their own weight. *If you were as strong as these ants, could you lift an elephant?*

124

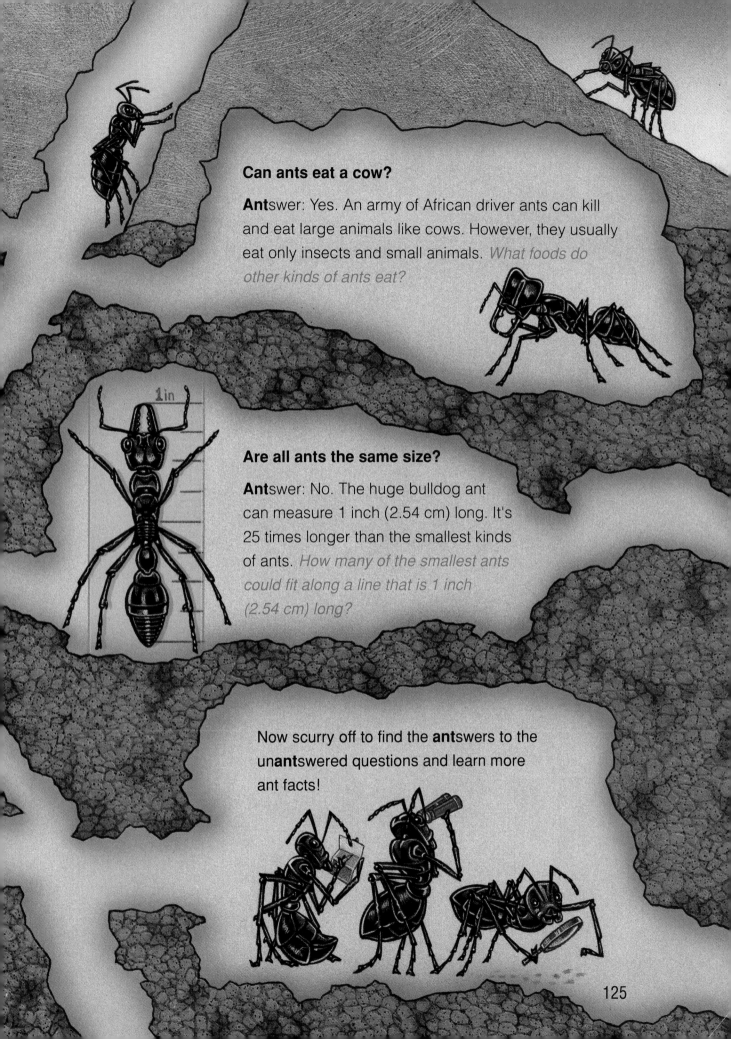

## Can ants eat a cow?

**Ant**swer: Yes. An army of African driver ants can kill and eat large animals like cows. However, they usually eat only insects and small animals. *What foods do other kinds of ants eat?*

## Are all ants the same size?

**Ant**swer: No. The huge bulldog ant can measure 1 inch (2.54 cm) long. It's 25 times longer than the smallest kinds of ants. *How many of the smallest ants could fit along a line that is 1 inch (2.54 cm) long?*

Now scurry off to find the **ant**swers to the un**ant**swered questions and learn more ant facts!

# MEET

## ARLINE AND JOSEPH BAUM

Arline and Joseph Baum are a husband-and-wife team who are fascinated by the art of illusion. Arline Baum once worked as an assistant to a magician. Joseph Baum was an art director for an advertising agency. His ability to create illusions with art won him many awards.

In *Opt: An Illusionary Tale,* the Baums have created a land of optical illusions. The book begins like this: "Seeing is believing, but sometimes our eyes deceive us. When this happens, it is called an optical illusion. Opt is a land of optical illusions." This book won an award for being an outstanding science trade book.

AN ILLUSIONARY TALE

OPT

BY ARLINE AND JOSEPH BAUM

# A Sunny Day in Opt, a day of banners, balloons, and surprises

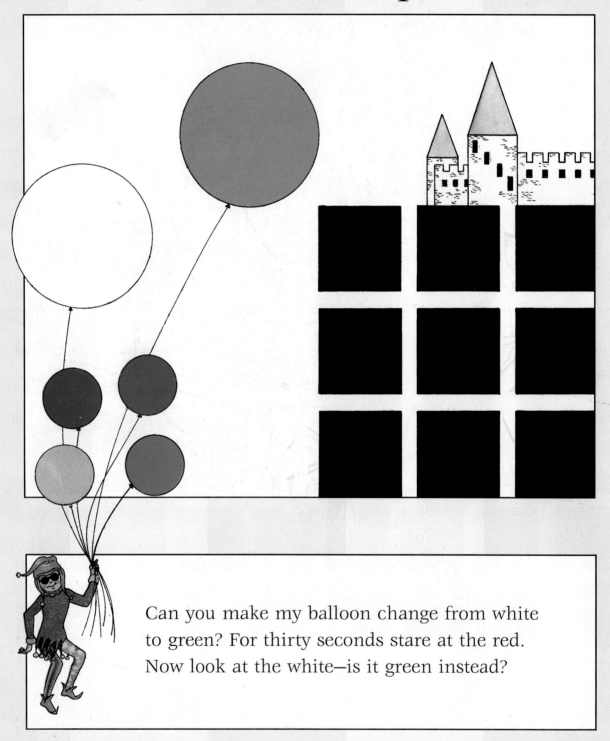

Can you make my balloon change from white to green? For thirty seconds stare at the red. Now look at the white—is it green instead?

# The Wall surrounding the castle

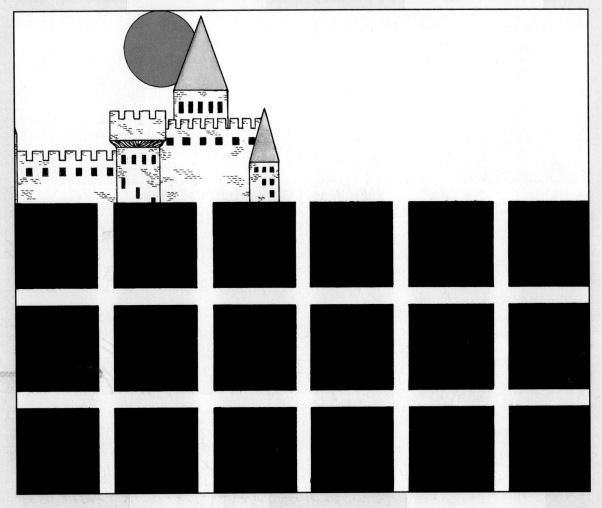

Where white lines cross, gray dots are seen.
One disappears where one has been.

# The Castle Guard with his trident

How many prongs do you see?
I see two on the bottom—but on the top, three.

# The Royal Messenger arriving with a letter for the King

The vertical lines of the messenger's cloak are crooked.
The red tape on the letter is longer than the blue.
But is this really true?
Remember, now you are in OPT!

# The Trumpeters announcing the arrival of the messenger

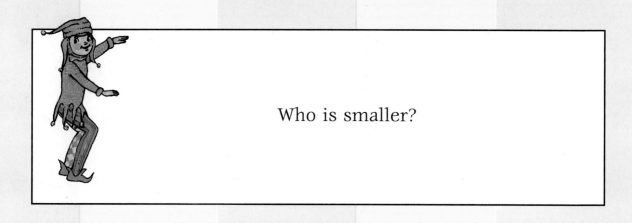

Who is smaller?

# The King and Queen waiting for the message

Who is taller?

# The Message for the King to read

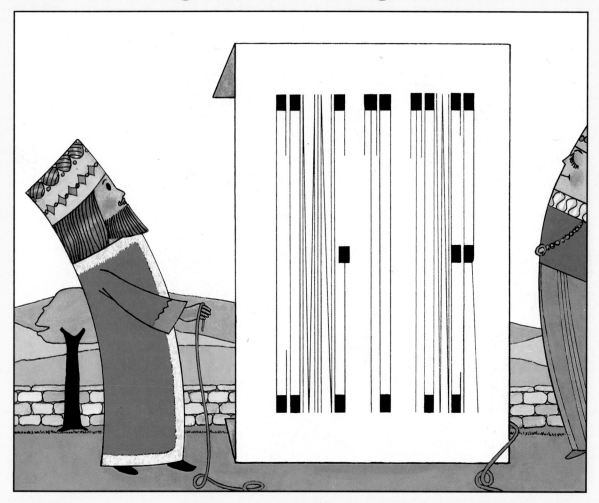

A clue to make the message clear.
First tilt the book, then take a look.
Who sent the message?

# The Royal Art Gallery, dusted and tidied

Are the top of the lampshade and the top of the lamp base the same length?
Two ladies framed—or is it four?
Hidden elsewhere, you'll see two more.

# The Prince goes fishing with his new rod

Which is the rod and which the branch of the tree?
Now look at the Prince's shirt.
What do you see?
Is the space between the shirt's black dots
larger than those same black spots?

# The Princess picking a special bouquet

Flowers fair, flowers bright.
Which flower center is larger—
the black or the white?

# The Great Hall, ready for the party

Should the Queen straighten the mirror on the wall?
There are eight more faces.
Can you find them all?

# The Opt Sign pointing the way to the zoo

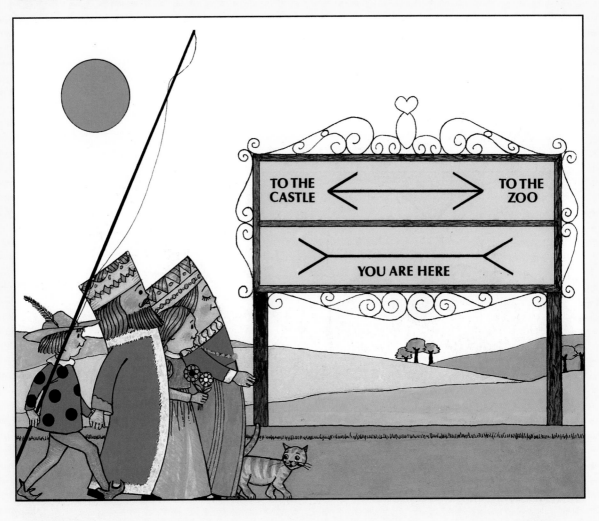

By the sign the royal family will stop.
Which line is longer, the bottom or top?
The King knows who the guest will be.
So do I—just follow me.

# The Opt Zoo, home of amazing animals

Faces within faces can be found—
if you just turn the book around.
Is the body of the royal pet shorter than its neck?
Is the height of the zookeeper's hat the same as

# The Zookeeper and the Royal Pet hearing the news

the width of its brim?
For thirty seconds stare at the star that is blue.
Now look at white paper—a colorful change,
just for you.

# The Pavilion decorated with banners

Are the banners light green or dark green,
light pink or dark pink?
Some say they're the same shade.
But what do *you* think?

# The Tower with guard spotting the guest

The guard marches up, stair by stair—
but is he getting anywhere?
He sees the guest.
Who can it be?
Turn the page and you will see!

# The Guest is here!

The fire-snorting dragon now comes in.
Turn the book and his eyes will spin.
Arriving with presents—and none too late.
But did he tie the red ribbons on straight?

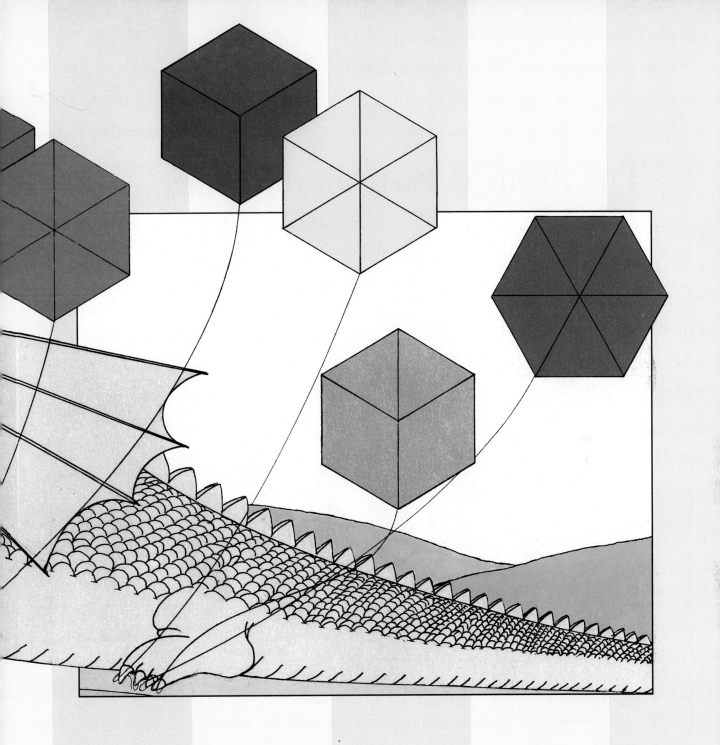

Look closely at the bright kites in the air.
Do flat kites or box kites float up there?

# The Birthday Party for the Prince

This gift, unwrapped, tells the Prince's age.
This is what the dragon said,
"Six blocks become seven if you stand on your head.
HAPPY BIRTHDAY!"

# The Dragon saying good-bye

The dragon was a perfect guest.
The party was a great success.
But *you* don't have to go away,
come join me in Opt any day.

147

# Houses

Houses are faces
(haven't you found?)
with their hats in the air,
and their necks in the ground.

Windows are noses,
windows are eyes,
and doors are the mouths
of a suitable size.

And a porch—or the place
where porches begin—
is just like a mustache
shading the chin.

Aileen Fisher

**Home Place**
by Crescent Dragonwagon,
illustrated by
Jerry Pinkney,
Macmillan,
1990

We're not
sure if we're
making her
up, or if
we really
can see
her. . . .

**Outside and
Inside You**
by Sandra Markle,
Bradbury Press, 1991

A building has a strong
framework to
support it.
You have a
framework,
too. Yours
is a bony
skeleton.
Without it,
you would not
have any
shape at all.

# OPENERS!

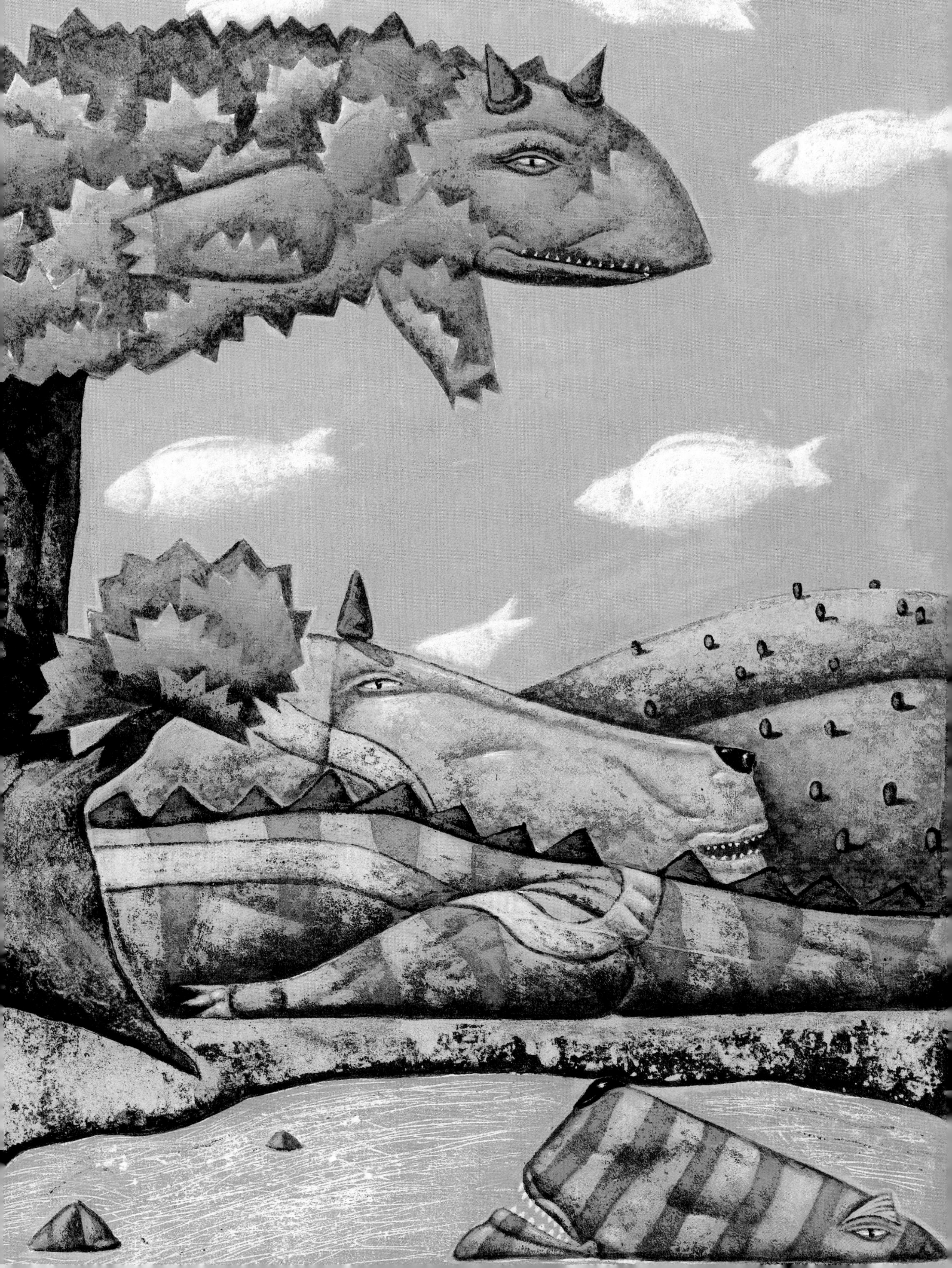

# Grandfather Tang's Story

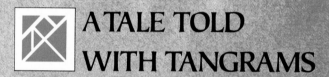

## A TALE TOLD WITH TANGRAMS

by ANN TOMPERT

illustrated by ED YOUNG

*Grandfather Tang and Little Soo were sitting under a peach tree in their backyard. They were amusing each other by making different shapes with their tangram puzzles.*

*"Let's do a story about the fox fairies," said Little Soo. So Grandfather Tang arranged his seven tangram pieces into the shape of a fox.*

*Then Grandfather Tang made another fox with Little Soo's seven tangram pieces. Little Soo clapped her hands as her grandfather began.*

Although Chou and Wu Ling were best friends, they were always trying to outdo each other. One day this rivalry almost brought their friendship to a tragic end. They were sitting under their favorite willow tree beside a river talking about their magic powers.

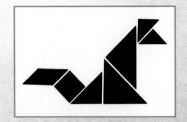

"I can change myself into a rabbit as quick as a wink," boasted Wu Ling. "I'll bet you can't do that."

"I can too," said Chou.

"Can not," said Wu Ling. "Anyway, actions speak louder than words." And he changed himself into a

**RABBIT.**

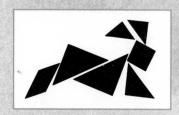

"Not bad," said Chou, smoothing his whiskers. "But watch me do better than that."

And before Wu Ling could blink, Chou changed from a fox into a

## DOG!

Now, when Chou changed himself into a dog, he not only looked like a dog, but he felt like a dog and acted like a dog. He bared his teeth and lashed his tail. Wu Ling shivered and twitched his nose.

"I love rabbits," Chou growled, "and I'm going to get you and gobble you up."

The dog edged closer and closer. Wu Ling's eyes grew bigger and bigger. He was too frightened to move at first. But then he thought, "I'll be safe if I can climb up the willow tree."

His little puff of a tail grew long and bushy and his tall ears shrunk as Wu Ling transformed himself into a

**SQUIRREL.**

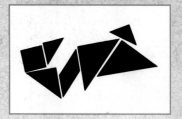

Wu Ling sprang into the willow tree and scrambled to the top.

"Chou will probably turn himself into a cat so he can climb up the tree after me," Wu Ling said to himself. "But he'll never catch me. I'll jump from tree to tree, and he won't be able to follow me."

Of course, Chou thought about changing himself into a cat.

"But that's just what Wu Ling expects me to do," he said to himself. "What can I do to surprise him?"

He thought and thought.

"I know. I'll swoop down upon him from above."

And he turned himself into a

## HAWK.

Chou circled round and round in the sky above the willow tree, searching for Wu Ling. Wu Ling peered through the leaves of the tree, looking for Chou on the ground.

Round and round Chou circled the willow tree until he spied Wu Ling.

"*Kek! Kek! Kek!*" he shrieked as he zoomed down upon the squirrel.

Wu Ling trembled. Chou's beak looked sharp enough to pierce right through him.

"If only I lived in a shell house," he thought. "Then Chou couldn't hurt me."

Chou stuck out his fierce claws to seize Wu Ling, but Wu Ling dove toward the river below the willow tree. And as he dove he tucked in his head and tail and legs, turned green, and changed into a

## TURTLE.

Wu Ling climbed up on a mossy rock in the middle of the river. He thought he was safe because he looked as if he were a part of the rock. Chou circled round and round, searching and searching, until his sharp eyes spotted the turtle. Then he swooped down, down, down toward him.

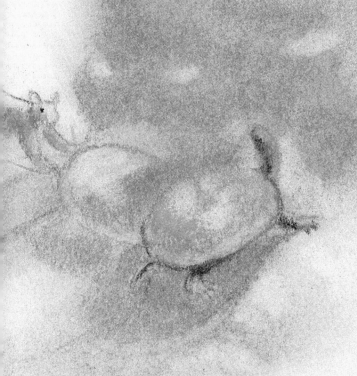

But just as Chou reached him, Wu Ling plunged into the water.

"Follow me and you'll drown," he cried.

"Don't worry," cried Chou, plunging right behind Wu Ling. His body grew longer, covered with scales. He whipped the water with his long, wicked tail. And he snapped his spike-toothed jaws as he turned into a

**CROCODILE.**

Wu Ling circled round and round as he plunged down, down, down to the bottom of the river. Chou lashed his wicked tail as he plunged after Wu Ling. Just as they reached the bottom, Chou clamped Wu Ling in his spike-toothed mouth.

"Now, I've got you!" he bellowed through his clenched teeth.

"Oh, no, you haven't," cried Wu Ling, who grew smaller and smaller and changed himself from green to gold as he transformed himself into a

**GOLDFISH.**

And he swam out of Chou's mouth
between his spiked teeth.

Then he hid in a patch of cattails.
Chou churned the water with his
lashing tail as he charged into the
patch after Wu Ling. With his head
swinging back and forth and his
eyes darting here and there,
he searched for Wu Ling.
Wu Ling knew that Chou
would not give up until
he found him.

"I must fly from here,"
he thought.

And he started to
honk as he transformed
himself into a

**GOOSE.**

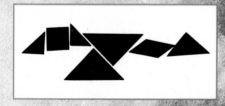

Chou charged after him, but Wu Ling spread his wings and took to the air.

Chou watched him fly to a small island where a flock of geese were feeding. By now he was not only very angry, he was also very hungry. He decided that if he could not catch Wu Ling, any goose would make him a good dinner. He splashed through the water toward the island until he reached it.

"*Honk! Honk! Honk!*" called Wu Ling.

And he took to the air.

A chorus of honks swelled the air as the flock of geese spread their wings to follow him. While Chou watched, the honking grew fainter, the flock grew smaller, and he felt his anger slowly drain away.

"Why, oh, why did we play that stupid game?" he moaned. "I'll never see Wu Ling again."

He closed his eyes and sank toward the river's bottom. Just as he touched it, however, he had an idea. And up he popped again, a goose himself.

Moments later, Chou was flying after Wu Ling and the other geese. He could hardly see or hear them at first. But he did not let this discourage him. Calling upon every last bit of his strength, he forged ahead.

Each flap of his wings brought him closer. The wedge of geese slowly grew bigger. The honking grew louder. At last Chou found himself flying beside Wu Ling.

"I'm tired of our silly game," he cried. "Come back with me to our willow tree."

Before Wu Ling could answer, something stung
Chou's right wing. He sank toward the ground.

165

A hunter had shot him. Wu Ling flew down beside Chou, placed his left wing under Chou's smashed right wing, and together they fluttered down to the edge of the forest.

The hunter ran toward them.

"Fly away," Chou urged Wu Ling. "Save yourself. Fly! Fly!"

"I won't desert you," cried Wu Ling.

And with a mighty roar, he changed into a

**LION.**

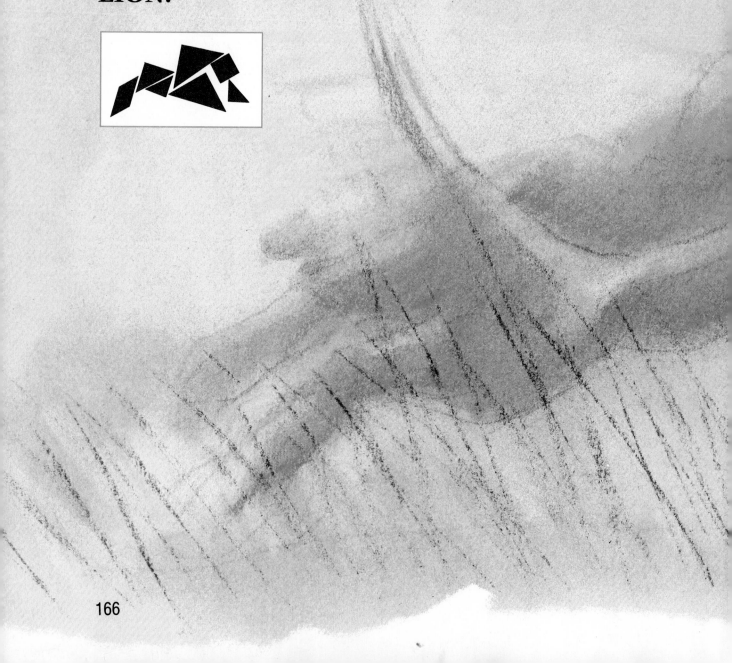

The hunter raised his bow. Wu Ling sprang toward him and knocked the bow from his hand. The hunter fled, leaving his bow behind.

Wu Ling and Chou returned to their fox shapes. And Wu Ling helped Chou to his den, where he took care of him until he was mended.

"Did they ever play that game again?" asked Little Soo.

"Many times," said her grandfather. "But they were very, very careful."

"That was a good story," said Little Soo. "Let's do another."

Grandfather arranged his seven tangram pieces.

"Is this story going to be about a man?" asked Little Soo.

"Yes," said her grandfather. "He's old and he's tired. He wants to sit under a tree and rest awhile."

"Is he a grandfather like you?" asked Little Soo.

"Yes," said her grandfather. "Just like me."

Little Soo arranged the seven pieces of her tangram beside her grandfather's.

"Is that a little girl?" he asked.

"Yes," said Little Soo. "Just like me. She'll sit and rest beside the man."

"That will make him very happy," said Grandfather Tang. "And now, Little Soo, what will we do?"

"We'll sit and rest together until Mother calls us for supper," said Little Soo.

"That will make me very happy," said her grandfather.

# MEET *Ann Tompert*

Ann Tompert used to dream about becoming an author. Before she went about making her dream come true, she taught school for a number of years. Now she has published about two dozen books. Her book *Little Fox Goes to the End of the World* was chosen as an American Library Association Notable Book. Tompert often writes about foxes, because she thinks that they have not been treated very well in literature.

Ann Tompert became interested in tangrams when she saw some books about them in a catalog. She sent for the books and became so fascinated by them that she began to make up her own tangrams, which led her to write *Grandfather Tang's Story.*

# PUZZLE

Map of a city with streets meeting at center?

Net to catch people jumping from a burning building?

Spider's web?

Burner on an electric stove?

Fingerprint?

No.

Frozen puddle after a hit by a rock.

# A SEEING POEM

A SEEING POEM HAPPENS WHEN WORDS TAKE A SHAPE THAT HELPS THEM TO TURN ON A LIGHT IN SOMEONE'S MIND

**Robert Froman**

# Meet
# Alison Alexander and Susie Bower

▶ Can science be fun? To Alison Alexander and Susie Bower, it's more than fun—it's magic! A few years ago, Alexander, a science teacher, and Bower, a journalist, decided to help their own children discover more about science. They put their heads together and created some amazing science experiments just for kids. The result was *Science Magic*. Alexander and Bower believe that anyone can become a science magician with the help of a few simple materials.

172

# SCIENCE MAGIC

### by Alison Alexander and Susie Bower

Science helps us learn about nature. Magic tries to make us believe that things are not always what they seem to be. This next selection mixes both. The result? Some experiments that challenge what we see.

173

# On a Sunny Day Make a Rainbow

**You will need:**
- mirror
- bright sunshine
- small mixing bowl (the size of the bowl will depend on the size of your mirror)

**1** Fill the bowl half way with water and place it near a window in direct sun.

Hold the mirror in the water at an angle so that the sun shines directly onto it. You will have to move the mirror gently about until the colors of the rainbow begin to appear on the wall.

**2** Lean the mirror against the side of the bowl without disturbing the water too much. When the water stops moving, you should be able to see the colors of the rainbow—red, orange, yellow, green, blue, indigo, violet. As the sun goes behind a cloud, the colors will fade.

You can make a rainbow in the garden. Wait until the sun begins to go down and then stand with your back to the sun and spray a shower of water through a hose pipe. As the sun shines on the water drops, the colors of the rainbow appear in the spray.

Although you cannot see it, a beam of light is made up from a mixture of all the colors of the rainbow. When the beam hits the water, each color is bent at a different angle. This means the beam of light is split up into separate beams of colored light. The mirror reflects these colors on to the wall where you can see red, orange, yellow, green, blue, indigo, and violet.

If you use a hose, the drops of water from the spray bend the beam of light and split it up into colors in the same way as the water in the bowl does. This forms a rainbow.

175

# Watch the Colors Disappear

**You will need:**
- ► colored crayons or paints
- ► scissors
- ► cardboard
  (cereal packet is fine)
- ► ruler
- ► jam jar lid
- ► large-eyed needle
  (wool needle is ideal)
- ► length of wool about 3 feet
  (1 meter) long

**1** ▶ Draw a circle on the cardboard using the jam jar lid and cut it out.

**2** ▶ Find the center by cutting a similar-sized circle in paper and folding it into quarters. Open it out and the point where the lines cross is the center.

**3** ▶ Mark the center of the cardboard circle. Divide the circle into six parts and color each section differently using the colors of the rainbow— red, orange, yellow, green, blue, violet. You can color the sections using just red, blue, green, red, blue, green.

**4** With the needle or the point of the scissors, make two small holes either side of the center of the circle, one-half inch (1 cm) apart. Thread the wool through both holes and knot the ends together to make a loop.

**5** Put one finger in each loop and twist up the wool by spinning your hands round. By moving your hands together and apart again you can make the disc spin. All the colors will disappear as the disc spins, and it will look as though it is white.

When the disc is spinning, all the colors go round very fast. You see them all at the same time and your eyes cannot see each different color separately. So you think the disc has no color at all and, to your eyes, it looks white.

177

# Make a Kaleidoscope

**You will need:**
- ▶ 2 handbag mirrors the same size (oblong are best)
- ▶ a piece of cardboard the same size as the mirrors
- ▶ greaseproof paper
- ▶ plastic wrap
- ▶ cellophane tape
- ▶ scissors
- ▶ small shapes of colored paper, beads, tin foil, or other tiny objects

**1** ▶ Lay the cardboard on the table and place the mirrors face down on either side of it. Tape them all together.

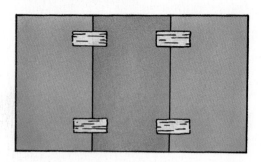

**2** ▶ Turn over the mirrors and cardboard and bend the mirrors together to make a triangle, so that the mirrors are inside the triangle. Tape them together.

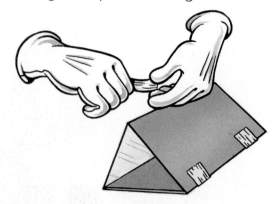

**3** ▶ Tape the greaseproof paper tightly across one end of the kaleidoscope.

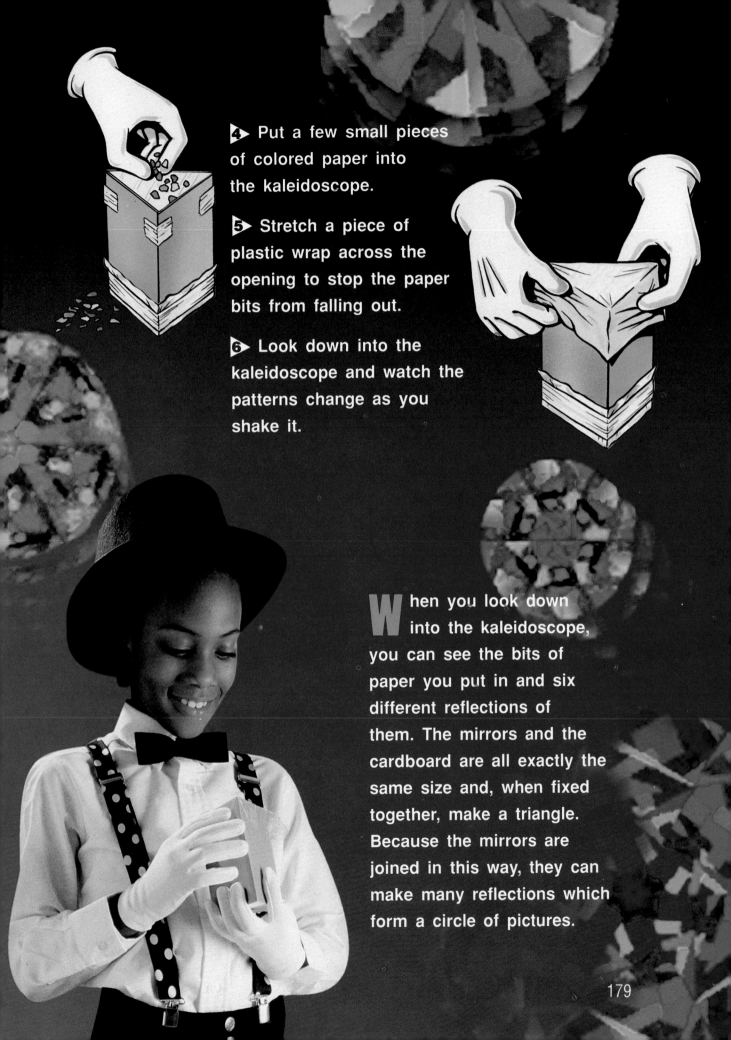

4▶ Put a few small pieces of colored paper into the kaleidoscope.

5▶ Stretch a piece of plastic wrap across the opening to stop the paper bits from falling out.

6▶ Look down into the kaleidoscope and watch the patterns change as you shake it.

When you look down into the kaleidoscope, you can see the bits of paper you put in and six different reflections of them. The mirrors and the cardboard are all exactly the same size and, when fixed together, make a triangle. Because the mirrors are joined in this way, they can make many reflections which form a circle of pictures.

179

# Peek Around the Corner with a Periscope

**You will need:**
► nail scissors
► 2 handbag mirrors (square ones are best)
► ruler
► oblong cracker box
► cellophane tape
► pencil

**1►** Near the top of the one side of the box, measure a 2-inch (5 cm) square window and cut it out. On the same side cut a slit 2 inches (5 cm) from the bottom of the box, as in the drawing.

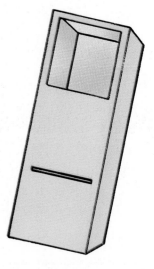

**2►** Turn the box around and on the opposite side cut another 2-inch (5 cm) square window near the bottom of the box. Cut a slit 2 inches (5 cm) from the top, as in the drawing. (It doesn't matter if your windows are not completely square.) Slide a mirror through each slit and place it diagonally between the slit and window. The top mirror must face downwards and the bottom mirror upwards.

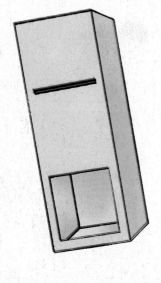

**3►** Tape the mirrors to the box. The edges may jut out of the slits.

180

**4▶** Sit under the table and hold the periscope so that one window is above the table top. Look through the bottom mirror and you will be able to see what is on the table. You can also use the periscope to peek around a corner or over the heads of a crowd of people.

**W**hen the end of a periscope is pointed round a corner, the view will be reflected in the top mirror. The two mirrors in the periscope are fixed facing each other, and they slope at the same angle. This means that the bottom mirror will reflect the view from the top mirror. By looking in the bottom mirror, you can see the hidden view.

# Acrobatic Pictures

**You will need:**
- ► a small notebook or some sheets of paper folded up to make a booklet
- ► pencils

**1** ► In the top right-hand corner of each page, draw a ball, changing its position a little every time. Bend the corner of the book back and flick the pages. The ball will bounce up and down on the page.

**2** ► You can turn the ball into a face with sad and happy expressions. You can also draw pin men jumping up and down. But you must remember to change the picture slightly each time.

The pictures flick past your eyes too quickly to see them separately. As the ball is in a slightly different position in each picture, it appears as if the ball is bouncing up and down.

# SUNFLAKES

If sunlight fell like snowflakes,

gleaming yellow and so bright,

we could build a sunman,

we could have a sunball fight,

we could watch the sunflakes

drifting in the sky.

We could go sleighing

in the middle of July

through sundrifts and sunbanks,

we could ride a sunmobile,

and we could touch sunflakes—

I wonder how they'd feel.

*Frank Asch*

# CONTENTS

# FAMILY TIES

So many groups in the family soup,
So many combinations,
Might be people who look like you
or they might be no relation!
Birds of a feather, they flock together,
Yes, sometimes they do.
But if a little bird joins an elephant herd,
Hey, that's a family, too!

from the song, "Free To Be . . . a Family"
LYRICS BY SARAH DURKEE

## ◆ MEET ◆
# VALERIE FLOURNOY

Valerie Flournoy was thinking about the members of her own family when she wrote *The Patchwork Quilt*. She was especially remembering her Grandma Buchanan and how much fun they had had together when Valerie was growing up.

Flournoy hopes children who read her story will have respect "not only for their own parents and grandparents but for all of their 'family'—their ancestors—who have gone before them."

# · THE ·
# PATCHWORK QUILT

by VALERIE FLOURNOY
pictures by JERRY PINKNEY

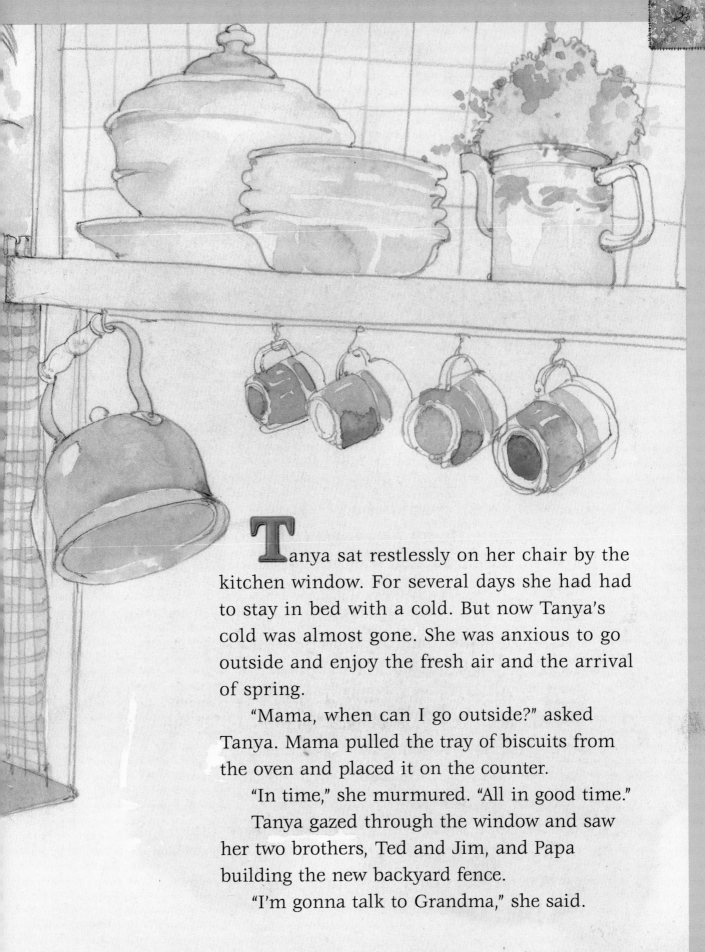

anya sat restlessly on her chair by the kitchen window. For several days she had had to stay in bed with a cold. But now Tanya's cold was almost gone. She was anxious to go outside and enjoy the fresh air and the arrival of spring.

"Mama, when can I go outside?" asked Tanya. Mama pulled the tray of biscuits from the oven and placed it on the counter.

"In time," she murmured. "All in good time."

Tanya gazed through the window and saw her two brothers, Ted and Jim, and Papa building the new backyard fence.

"I'm gonna talk to Grandma," she said.

Grandma was sitting in her favorite spot—the big soft chair in front of the picture window. In her lap were scraps of materials of all textures and colors. Tanya recognized some of them. The plaid was from Papa's old work shirt, and the red scraps were from the shirt Ted had torn that winter.

"Whatcha gonna do with all that stuff?" Tanya asked.

"Stuff? These ain't stuff. These little pieces gonna make me a quilt, a patchwork quilt."

Tanya tilted her head. "I know what a quilt is, Grandma. There's one on your bed, but it's old and dirty and Mama can never get it clean."

Grandma sighed. "It ain't dirty, honey. It's worn, the way it's supposed to be."

Grandma flexed her fingers to keep them from stiffening. She sucked in some air and said, "My mother made me a quilt when I wasn't any older than you. But sometimes the old ways are forgotten."

Tanya leaned against the chair and rested her head on her grandmother's shoulder.

Just then Mama walked in with two glasses of milk and some biscuits. Mama looked at the scraps of material that were scattered all over. "Grandma," she said, "I just cleaned this room, and now it's a mess."

"It's not a mess, Mama," Tanya said through a mouthful of biscuit. "It's a quilt."

"A quilt! You don't need these scraps. I can get you a quilt," Mama said.

Grandma looked at her daughter and then turned to her grandchild. "Yes, your mama can get you a quilt from any department store. But it won't be like my patchwork quilt, and it won't last as long either."

Mama looked at Grandma, then picked up Tanya's empty glass and went to make lunch.

Grandma's eyes grew dark and distant. She turned away from Tanya and gazed out the window, absent-mindedly rubbing the pieces of material through her fingers.

"Grandma, I'll help you make your quilt," Tanya said.

"Thank you, honey."

"Let's start right now. We'll be finished in no time."

Grandma held Tanya close and patted her head. "It's gonna take quite a while to make this quilt, not a couple of days or a week—not even a month. A good quilt, a masterpiece . . ." Grandma's eyes shone at the thought. "Why I need more material. More gold and blue, some red and green. And I'll need the time to do it right. It'll take me a year at least."

"A year," shouted Tanya. "That's too long. I can't wait that long, Grandma."

Grandma laughed. "A year ain't that long, honey. Makin' this quilt gonna be a joy. Now run along and let Grandma rest." Grandma turned her head toward the sunlight and closed her eyes.

"I'm gonna make a masterpiece," she murmured, clutching a scrap of cloth in her hand, just before she fell asleep.

"We'll have to get you a new pair and use these old ones for rags," Mama said as she hung the last piece of wash on the clothesline one August afternoon.

Jim was miserable. His favorite blue corduroy pants had been held together with patches; now they were beyond repair.

"Bring them here," Grandma said.

Grandma took part of the pant leg and cut a few blue squares. Jim gave her a hug and watched her add his patches to the others.

"A quilt won't forget. It can tell your life story," she said.

The arrival of autumn meant school and Halloween. This year Tanya would be an African princess. She danced around in the long, flowing robes Mama had made from several yards of colorful material. The old bracelets and earrings Tanya had found in a trunk in the attic jingled noisily as she moved. Grandma cut some squares out of the leftover scraps and added Tanya to the quilt too!

The days grew colder but Tanya and her brothers didn't mind. They knew snow wasn't far away. Mama dreaded winter's coming. Every year she would plead with Grandma to move away from the drafty window, but Grandma wouldn't budge.

"Grandma, please," Mama scolded. "You can sit here by the heater."

"I'm not your grandmother, I'm your mother," Grandma said. "And I'm gonna sit here in the Lord's light and make my masterpiece."

It was the end of November when Ted, Jim, and Tanya got their wish. They awoke one morning to find everything in sight covered with snow. Tanya got dressed and flew down the stairs. Ted and Jim, and even Mama and Papa, were already outside.

"I don't like leaving Grandma in that house by herself," Mama said. "I know she's lonely."

Tanya pulled herself out of the snow being careful not to ruin her angel. "Grandma isn't lonely," Tanya said happily. "She and the quilt are telling each other stories."

Mama glanced questioningly at Tanya, "Telling each other stories?"

"Yes, Grandma says a quilt never forgets!"

The family spent the morning and most of the afternoon sledding down the hill. Finally, when they were all numb from the cold, they went inside for hot chocolate and sandwiches.

"I think I'll go sit and talk to Grandma," Mama said.

"Then she can explain to you about our quilt— our very own family quilt," Tanya said.

Mama saw the mischievous glint in her youngest child's eyes.

"Why, I may just have her do that, young lady," Mama said as she walked out of the kitchen.

Tanya leaned over the table to see into the living room. Grandma was hunched over, her eyes close to the fabric as she made tiny stitches. Mama sat at the old woman's feet. Tanya couldn't hear what was said but she knew Grandma was telling Mama all about quilts and how *this* quilt would be very special. Tanya sipped her chocolate slowly, then she saw Mama pick up a piece of fabric, rub it with her fingers, and smile.

From that moment on both women spent their winter evenings working on the quilt. Mama did the sewing while Grandma cut the fabrics and placed the scraps in a pattern of colors. Even while they were cooking and baking all their Christmas specialties during the day, at night they still worked on the quilt. Only once did Mama put it aside. She wanted to wear something special Christmas night, so she bought some gold material and made a beautiful dress. Tanya knew without asking that the gold scraps would be in the quilt too.

There was much singing and laughing that Christmas. All Grandma's sons and daughters and nieces and nephews came to pay their respects. The Christmas tree lights shone brightly, filling the room with sparkling colors. Later, when everyone had gone home, Papa said he had never felt so much happiness in the house. And Mama agreed.

When Tanya got downstairs the next morning, she found Papa fixing pancakes.

"Is today a special day too?" asked Jim.

"Where's Mama?" asked Tanya.

"Grandma doesn't feel well this morning," Papa said. "Your mother is with her now till the doctor gets here."

"Will Grandma be all right?" Ted asked.

Papa rubbed his son's head and smiled. "There's nothing for you to worry about. We'll take care of Grandma."

Tanya looked into the living room. There on the back of the big chair rested the patchwork quilt. It was folded neatly, just as Grandma had left it.

"Mother didn't want us to know she wasn't feeling well. She thought it would spoil our Christmas," Mama told them later, her face drawn and tired, her eyes a puffy red. "Now it's up to all of us to be quiet and make her as comfortable as possible." Papa put an arm around Mama's shoulder.

"Can we see Grandma?" Tanya asked.

"No, not tonight," Papa said. "Grandma needs plenty of rest."

It was nearly a week, the day before New Year's, before the children were permitted to see their grandmother. She looked tired and spoke in whispers.

"We miss you, Grandma," Ted said.

"And your muffins and hot chocolate," added Jim. Grandma smiled.

"Your quilt misses you too, Grandma," Tanya said. Grandma's smile faded from her lips. Her eyes grew cloudy.

"My masterpiece," Grandma sighed. "It would have been beautiful. Almost half finished." The old woman closed her eyes and turned away from her grandchildren. Papa whispered it was time to leave. Ted, Jim, and Tanya crept from the room.

Tanya walked slowly to where the quilt lay. She had seen Grandma and Mama work on it. Tanya thought real hard. She knew how to cut the scraps, but she wasn't certain of the rest. Just then Tanya felt a hand resting on her shoulder. She looked up and saw Mama.

"Tomorrow," Mama said.

New Year's Day was the beginning. After the dishes were washed and put away, Tanya and Mama examined the quilt.

"You cut more squares, Tanya, while I stitch some patches together," Mama said.

Tanya snipped and trimmed the scraps of material till her hands hurt from the scissors. Mama watched her carefully, making sure the squares were all the same size. The next day was the same as the last. More snipping and cutting. But Mama couldn't always be around to watch Tanya work. Grandma had to be looked after. So Tanya worked by herself. Then one night, as Papa read them stories, Jim walked over and looked at the quilt. In it he saw patches of blue. His blue. Without saying a word Jim picked up the scissors and some scraps and started to make squares. Ted helped Jim put the squares in piles while Mama showed Tanya how to join them.

Every day, as soon as she got home from school, Tanya worked on the quilt. Ted and Jim were too busy with sports, and Mama was looking after Grandma, so Tanya worked alone. But after a few weeks she stopped. Something was wrong—something was missing, Tanya thought. For days the quilt lay on the back of the chair. No one knew why Tanya had stopped working. Tanya would sit and look at the quilt. Finally she knew. Some*thing* wasn't missing. Some*one* was missing from the quilt.

That evening before she went to bed Tanya tiptoed into Grandma's room, a pair of scissors in her hand. She quietly lifted the end of Grandma's old quilt and carefully removed a few squares.

February and March came and went as Mama proudly watched her daughter work on the last few rows of patches. Tanya always found time for the quilt. Grandma had been watching too. The old woman had been getting stronger and stronger as the months passed. Once she was able, Papa would carry Grandma to her chair by the window. "I needs the Lord's light," Grandma said. Then she would sit and hum softly to herself and watch Tanya work.

"Yes, honey, this quilt is nothin' but a joy," Grandma said.

Summer vacation was almost here. One June day Tanya came home to find Grandma working on the quilt again! She had finished sewing the last few squares together; the stuffing was in place, and she was already pinning on the backing.

"Grandma!" Tanya shouted.

Grandma looked up. "Hush, child. It's almost time to do the quilting on these patches. But first I have some special finishing touches . . ."

The next night Grandma cut the final thread with her teeth. "There. It's done," she said. Mama helped Grandma spread the quilt full length.

Nobody had realized how big it had gotten or how beautiful. Reds, greens, blues, and golds, light shades and dark, blended in and out throughout the quilt.

"It's beautiful," Papa said. He touched the gold patch, looked at Mama, and remembered. Jim remembered too. There was his blue and the red from Ted's shirt. There was Tanya's Halloween costume. And there was Grandma. Even though her patch was old, it fit right in.

They all remembered the past year. They especially remembered Tanya and all her work. So it had been decided. In the right hand corner of the last row of patches was delicately stitched, "For Tanya from your Mama and Grandma."

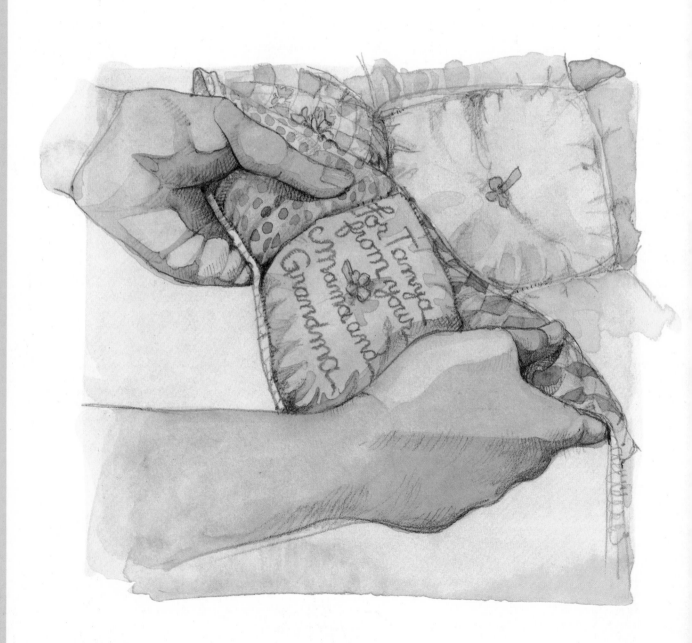

# ◆ MEET ◆
# JERRY PINKNEY

Jerry Pinkney's elementary school teachers often asked him to draw on the chalkboard for class projects. The artist says that this made him feel special, because he has loved to draw for as long as he can remember.

Today Jerry Pinkney spends much of his time in libraries. He looks for information to add just the right details to his illustrations. You can see some of these details in *The Patchwork Quilt,* which won the Coretta Scott King Award for Illustration. Among the many other books the artist has illustrated are *Rabbit Makes a Monkey of Lion* and *Turtle in July.*

# "Wood" You

Crowing rooster
by the Blas family

María Jiménez Ojeda
putting finishing
touches on a carving

# BELIEVE IT?

**D**ancing chickens! Purple lions! Kings and cactus! Where do they come from? How are they made?

Entire families in Mexico's Oaxaca Valley work together to produce these imaginative woodcarvings. With machetes and kitchen knives, some of the adults and teenagers carve the figures from copal wood. Younger children sand the figures smooth. At painting time, other members of the family take over. Even the family's farm animals help with the finishing touches. Trimmings from their hair are used to make tails, manes, and whiskers for the carvings.

Carving is not new to the Oaxacan people. For more than five hundred years, they have carved masks and miniature toys. What is new is that now people from other parts of the world are getting a chance to see and buy their woodcarvings.

*Patterned cat by Margarito Melchor*

*Two dancing chickens by Ventura Fabian*

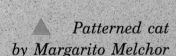

*Margarito Melchor Fuentes and his wife Maria Teresa Santiago working on two carvings*

# En un barrio de
# LOS ANGELES

## (IN A NEIGHBORHOOD IN LOS ANGELES)

| | |
|---|---|
| el español | I learned |
| lo aprendí | Spanish |
| de mi abuela | from my grandma |
| | |
| mijito | *mijito* |
| no llores | don't cry |
| me decía | she'd tell me |
| | |
| en las mañanas | on the mornings |
| cuando salían | my parents |
| mis padres | would leave |
| | |
| a trabajar | to work |
| en las canerías | at the fish |
| de pescado | canneries |
| | |
| mi abuela | my grandma |
| platicaba | would chat |
| con las sillas | with chairs |
| | |
| les cantaba | sing them |
| canciones | old |
| antiguas | songs |
| | |
| les bailaba | dance |
| valses en | waltzes with them |
| la cocina | in the kitchen |
| | |
| cuando decía | when she'd say |
| niño barrigón | *niño barrigón* |
| se reía | she'd laugh |

con mi abuela
aprendí
a contar nubes

with my grandma
I learned
to count clouds

a reconocer
en las macetas
la yerbabuena

to point out
in flowerpots
mint leaves

mi abuela
llevaba lunas
en el vestido

my grandma
wore moons
on her dress

la montaña
el desierto
el mar de México

Mexico's mountains
deserts
ocean

en sus ojos
yo los veía
en sus trenzas

in her eyes
I'd see them
in her braids

yo los tocaba
con su voz
yo los olía

I'd touch them
in her voice
smell them

un día
me dijeron:
se fue muy lejos

one day
I was told:
she went far away

pero yo aún
la siento
conmigo

but still
I feel her
with me

diciéndome
quedito al oído
mijito

whispering
in my ear
*mijito*

**Francisco X. Alarcón (translated by Francisco Aragon)**

すきやき

Ina R. Friedman

# How My Parents
# Learned to Eat

Illustrated by Allen Say

In our house, some days we eat with chopsticks and some days we eat with knives and forks.

For me, it's natural.

When my mother met my father, she was a Japanese schoolgirl and he was an American sailor. His ship was stationed in Yokohama.

Every day, my father, whose name is John, walked in the park with my mother, Aiko. They sat on a bench and talked. But my father was afraid to invite my mother to dinner.

If we go to a restaurant, he thought, I'll go hungry because I don't know how to eat with chopsticks. And if I go hungry, I'll act like a bear. Then Aiko won't like me. I'd better not ask her to dinner.

My mother wondered why my father never invited her to dinner. Perhaps John is afraid I don't know how to eat with a knife and fork and I'll look silly, she thought. Maybe it is best if he doesn't invite me to dinner.

So they walked and talked and never ate a bowl of rice or a piece of bread together.

One day, the captain of my father's ship said, "John, in three weeks the ship is leaving Japan."

My father was sad. He wanted to marry my mother. How can I ask her to marry me? he thought. I don't even know if we like the same food. And if we don't, we'll go hungry. It's hard to be happy if you're hungry. I'll have to find out what food she likes. And I'll have to learn to eat with chopsticks.

So he went to a Japanese restaurant.

Everyone sat on cushions around low tables. My father bowed to the waiter. "Please, teach me to eat with chopsticks."

"Of course," said the waiter, bowing.

The waiter brought a bowl of rice and a plate of sukiyaki. Sukiyaki is made of small pieces of meat, vegetables, and tofu. It smelled good. My father wanted to gobble it up.

The waiter placed two chopsticks between my father's fingers. "Hold the bottom chopstick still. Move the top one to pick up the food," the waiter said.

My father tried, but the meat slipped off his chopstick and fell on his lap.

The waiter came back with a bowl of soup. How can I eat soup with chopsticks? my father thought.

"Drink," said the waiter. "Drink from the bowl."

"Thank goodness," my father said. After the soup my father felt better. He picked up the chopsticks. Finally, my father put one piece of meat in his mouth. Delicious!

"More soup, please," he said.

After three bowls of soup my father felt much better. Then he practiced some more with his chopsticks. Soon, there was more sukiyaki in his belly than on the floor. But it was too late to call my mother. He had to run back to his ship.

That night, my mother was sad. Every other day my father had come to see her. That day he did not come. He did not call on the telephone. Perhaps he was tired of walking and talking. Perhaps he was ashamed of her because she did not know how to eat with a knife and fork. Perhaps his ship had sailed away. All night she could not sleep.

And all night my father sat on his bunk, pretending to pick up sukiyaki.

The next morning my father called my mother. "Please, will you eat dinner with me tonight?"

"Yes!" my mother shouted into the phone. First she was happy. Then she was afraid. She took her schoolbooks and ran to the house of Great Uncle.

Great Uncle had visited England. He had seen the British Museum. He had eaten dinners with Englishmen.

My mother knocked at the door. Great Uncle opened it. "Why are you so sad, child?" he asked.

"Because I must learn to eat with a knife and fork by seven o'clock tonight."

Great Uncle nodded. "Foreign ways are quite strange. Why do you want to eat with a knife and fork?"

My mother blushed.

"Is it the American sailor?" Great Uncle asked. "I see. . . . Here, take this note to your teacher. At lunchtime I will come and take you to a foreign restaurant. By seven o'clock tonight you will eat with a knife and fork."

My mother picked up her school bag and bowed.

"No," Great Uncle stuck out his hand. "In the West you shake hands."

The restaurant had red carpets and many lights. Great Uncle pulled out a chair for my mother. "In the West, men help ladies into chairs," he told her.

My mother looked at the small fork and the large fork on the left. She looked at the knife, little spoon, and big spoon on the right. Her head grew dizzy.

"Different utensils for different foods," Great Uncle said.

"How strange to dirty so many things," said my mother. "A chopstick is a chopstick. I can eat everything with two chopsticks."

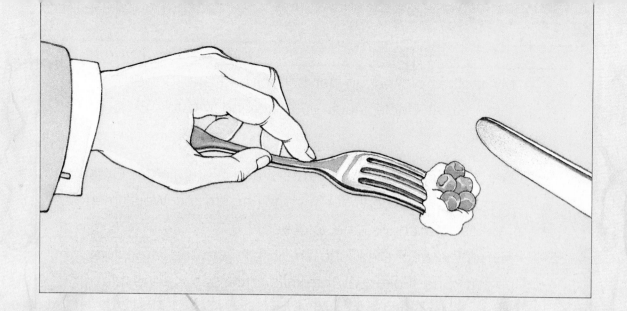

When the waiter brought the soup, Great Uncle pointed at the large spoon. "Dip it slowly, bring it to your mouth. Sip quietly."

My mother's hand trembled. The soup spilled onto the white cloth.

"You'll learn," Great Uncle encouraged her.

When my mother was finished with the soup, the waiter brought her a plate of mashed potatoes, roast beef, and peas.

"This is the way Westerners eat," Great Uncle said. "With the knife and fork they cut the meat. Then they hold the fork upside down in their left hand. Like birds, they build a nest of mashed potatoes. They put the peas in the nest with the knife. Then they slip the nest into their mouth. Try it."

The mashed potatoes were not difficult. But the peas rolled all over the plate. "Impossible," said my mother. "I'll never learn by seven o'clock tonight."

"You can learn anything," Great Uncle said. "Try again. More mashed potatoes and peas, please," he said to the waiter.

At seven o'clock my father came to see my mother.

"Why didn't you wear your kimono?" he asked. "We are going to a Japanese restaurant."

"A Japanese restaurant? Don't you think I know how to eat Western food?" my mother asked.

"Of course. Don't you think I know how to eat Japanese food?"

"Of course."

"Then, tonight we'll eat meat and potatoes. Tomorrow night we'll eat sukiyaki."

"Tomorrow night I will wear my kimono," my mother said. She started to bow. Then she stopped and put out her hand. My father shook it.

My father ordered two plates of mashed potatoes, roast beef, and peas. He watched my mother cut the meat into pieces. He stared when she turned over her fork and made a bird's nest. He was amazed.

"You are very clever with a knife and fork," he said.

"Thank you," said my mother.

"You must teach me," my father said. "That's a new way of eating peas."

"Teach you?"

"Yes, Americans don't eat that way." He slid his fork under some peas and put them in his mouth.

My mother stared at him. "But Great Uncle taught me. He lived in England. He knows the ways of the West."

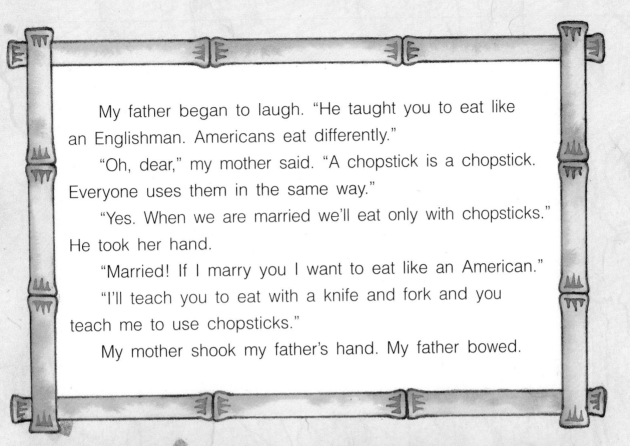

My father began to laugh. "He taught you to eat like an Englishman. Americans eat differently."

"Oh, dear," my mother said. "A chopstick is a chopstick. Everyone uses them in the same way."

"Yes. When we are married we'll eat only with chopsticks." He took her hand.

"Married! If I marry you I want to eat like an American."

"I'll teach you to eat with a knife and fork and you teach me to use chopsticks."

My mother shook my father's hand. My father bowed.

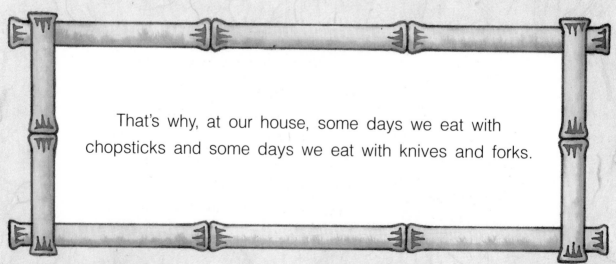

That's why, at our house, some days we eat with chopsticks and some days we eat with knives and forks.

# MEET
# INA R. FRIEDMAN

Sometimes a good friend can inspire a good book. Ina R. Friedman says, *"How My Parents Learned to Eat* grew out of my friendship with a Japanese woman who married an American. I thought how fortunate their children were to be brought up with two cultures."* Her story about how cultural understanding can start with everyday things won a Christopher Award.

# MEET
# ALLEN SAY

When Allen Say was twelve, a Japanese cartoonist taught him how to draw. Years later, Say drew pictures for many children's books. *How My Parents Learned to Eat* shows details that he remembered from growing up in Japan. *The Boy of the Three-Year Nap,* a Caldecott Honor Book, retells a Japanese folk tale. Say has said, "I look at my work as a personal tree-ring, a growth record."

# Family Albums

**CERTIFICATE OF BIRTH**
**THE NIX MEMORIAL HOSPITAL**
SAN ANTONIO, TEXAS

## Mom Can't See Me
by Sally Hobart Alexander
photographs by George Ancona
Macmillan, 1990

Once I put a scarf over my eyes and tried out being blind. I got lots of bumps just like Mom, so I took off the blindfold. Mom can't take off her blindness.

## Music, Music for Everyone

by Vera B. Williams
Mulberry Books, 1984

I brushed Grandma's hair and
told her my whole idea. She
thought it was a great idea.
"But tell the truth, Grandma,"
I begged her. "Do you think
kids could really do that?"

# RAMONA
# FOREVER

by Beverly Cleary

*It* has been a year of many changes for Ramona Quimby and her family. Aunt Bea and Uncle Hobart are newly married, and they are headed north on their honeymoon. Ramona and her sister, Beezus, have tied their white shoes to the truck's bumper for good luck.

The family cat, Picky-picky, has died suddenly, but there is good news, too. Mr. Quimby has started a new job as the manager of a large food store, and Mrs. Quimby is going to have a baby. The Quimbys have even given the baby a name—baby Algie.

Ramona has mixed feelings about all the changes, especially baby Algie. How will it feel not to be the youngest anymore?

After the wedding, everyone felt let down, the way they always felt the day after Christmas, only worse. Nothing seemed interesting after so much excitement. Grandpa Day had flown back to his sunshine and shuffleboard. Mr. Quimby was at work all day. Friends had gone off to camp, to the mountains, or the beach. Howie and Willa Jean had gone to visit their other grandmother.

"Girls, please stop moping around," said Mrs. Quimby.

"We can't find anything to do," said Beezus.

Ramona was silent. If she complained, her mother would tell her to clean out her closet.

"Read a book," said Mrs. Quimby. "Both of you, read a book."

"I've read all my books a million times," said Ramona, who usually enjoyed rereading her favorites.

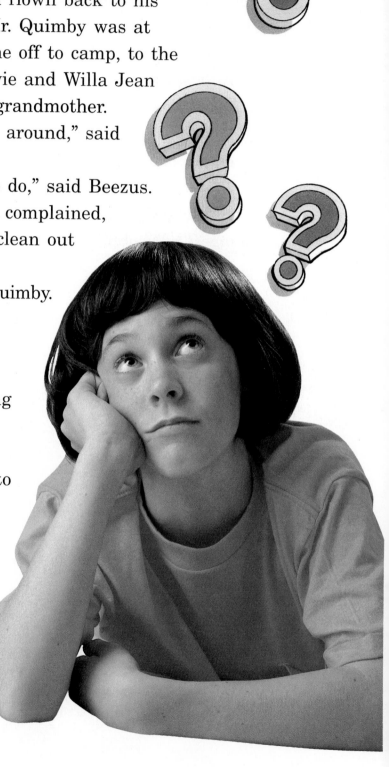

"Then go to the library." Mrs. Quimby was beginning to sound irritable.

"It's too hot," complained Ramona. Mrs. Quimby glanced at her watch.

"Mother, are you expecting someone?" asked Ramona. "You keep looking at your watch."

"I certainly am," said her mother. "A stranger." With a big sigh, Mrs. Quimby sank heavily to the couch, glanced at her watch again, and closed her eyes. The girls exchanged guilty looks. Their poor mother, worn out by Algie kicking her when there was so much of her to feel hot.

"Mother, are you all right?" Beezus sounded worried.

"I'm fine," snapped Mrs. Quimby, which surprised the girls into behaving.

That evening, the sisters helped their mother put together a cold supper of tuna fish salad and sliced tomatoes. While the family was eating, Mr. Quimby told them that now that the "Hawaiian Holidays" sale with bargains in fresh pineapple and papaya had come to an end, all the Shop-rite markets were preparing for "Western Bar-b-q Week" with specials on steak, baked beans, tomato sauce, and chili. He planned to paint bucking broncos on the front windows.

Mrs. Quimby nibbled at her salad and glanced at her watch.

"And everybody will see your paintings," said Ramona, happy that her father was now an artist as well as a market manager.

"Not quite the same as an exhibit in a museum," said Mr. Quimby, who did not sound as happy as Ramona expected.

Mrs. Quimby pushed her chair farther from the table and glanced at her watch. All eyes were on her.

"Shall I call the doctor?" asked Mr. Quimby.

"Please," said Mrs. Quimby as she rose from the table, hugged Algie, and breathed, "Oo-oo."

Ramona and Beezus, excited and frightened, looked at one another. At last! The fifth Quimby would soon be here. Nothing would be the same again, ever. Mr. Quimby reported that the doctor would meet them at the hospital. Without being asked, Beezus ran for the bag her mother had packed several weeks ago.

Mrs. Quimby kissed her daughters. "Don't look so frightened," she said. "Everything is going to be all right. Be good girls, and Daddy will be home as soon as he can." She bent forward and hugged Algie again.

The house suddenly seemed empty. The girls listened to the car back out of the driveway. The sound of the motor became lost in traffic.

"Well," said Beezus, "I suppose we might as well do the dishes."

"I suppose so." Ramona tested all the doors, including the door to the basement, to make sure they were locked.

"Too bad Picky-picky isn't here to eat all this tuna salad no one felt like eating." Beezus scraped the plates into the garbage.

To her own surprise, Ramona burst into tears and buried her face in a dish towel. "I just want Mother to come home," she wept.

Beezus wiped her soapy hands on the seat of her cutoff jeans. Then she put her arms around Ramona, something she had never done before. "Don't worry, Ramona. Everything will be all right. Mother said so, and I remember when you came."

Ramona felt better. A big sister could be a comfort if she wanted to.

"You got born and Mother was fine." Beezus handed Ramona a clean dish towel.

Minutes crawled by. The long Oregon dusk turned into night. The girls turned on the television set to a program about people in a hospital, running, shouting, giving orders. Quickly they turned it off. "I hope Aunt Bea and Uncle Hobart are all right," said Ramona. The girls longed for their loving aunt, who was cheerful in times of trouble and who was always there when the family needed her. Now she was in a truck, riding along the Canadian Highway to Alaska. Ramona thought about bears, mean bears. She wondered if two pairs of white shoes still danced from the bumper of the truck.

The ring of the telephone made Ramona feel as if arrows of electricity had shot through her stomach as Beezus ran to answer.

"Oh." There was disappointment in Beezus's voice. "All right, Daddy. No. No, we don't mind." When the conversation ended, she turned to Ramona, who was wild for news, and said, "Algie is taking his time. Daddy wants to stay with Mom and wanted to be sure we didn't mind staying alone. I said we didn't, and he said we were brave girls."

"Oh," said Ramona, who longed for her father's return. "Well, I'm brave, I guess." Even though the evening was unusually warm, she closed all the windows.

"I suppose we should go to bed," said Beezus. "If you want, you can get in bed with me.

"We better leave lights on for Daddy." Ramona turned on the porch light, as well as all the lights in the living room and hall, before she climbed into her sister's bed. "So Daddy won't fall over anything," she explained.

"Good idea," agreed Beezus. Each sister knew the other felt safer with the lights on.

"I hope Algie will hurry," said Ramona.

"So do I," agreed Beezus.

The girls slept lightly until the sound of a key in the door awoke them. "Daddy?" Beezus called out.

"Yes." Mr. Quimby came down the hall to the door of Beezus's room. "Great news.

Roberta Day Quimby, six pounds, four ounces, arrived safe and sound. Your mother is fine."

Barely awake, Ramona asked, "Who's Roberta?"

"Your new sister," answered her father, "and my namesake."

"*Sister*." Now Ramona was wide-awake. The family had referred to the baby as Algie so long she had assumed that of course she would have a brother.

"Yes, a beautiful little sister," said her father. "Now, go back to sleep. It's four o'clock in the morning, and I've got to get up at seven-thirty."

The next morning, Mr. Quimby overslept and ate his breakfast standing up. He was halfway out the door when he called back, "When I get off work, we'll have dinner at the Whopperburger, and then we'll all go see Roberta and your mother."

The day was long and lonely. Even a swimming lesson at the park and a trip to the library did little to make time pass. "I wonder what Roberta looks like?" said Beezus.

"And whose room she will share when she outgrows the bassinette?" worried Ramona.

The one happy moment in the day for the girls was a telephone call from their mother, who reported that Roberta was a beautiful, healthy little sister. She couldn't wait to bring her home, and she was proud of her daughters for being so good about staying alone. This pleased Beezus and Ramona so much they ran the vacuum cleaner and dusted, which made time pass faster until their father, looking exhausted, came home to take them out for hamburgers and a visit to the fifth Quimby.

Ramona could feel her heart pounding as she finally climbed the steps to the hospital. Visitors, some carrying flowers and others looking careworn, walked toward the elevators. Nurses hurried, a doctor was paged over the loudspeaker. Ramona could scarcely bear her own excitement. The rising of the elevator made her stomach feel as if it had stayed behind on the first floor. When the elevator stopped, Mr. Quimby led the way down the hall.

"Excuse me," called a nurse.

Surprised, the family stopped and turned.

"Children under twelve are not allowed to visit the maternity ward," said the nurse. "Little girl, you will have to go down and wait in the lobby."

"Why is that?" asked Mr. Quimby.

"Children under twelve might have contagious diseases," explained the nurse. "We have to protect the babies."

"I'm sorry, Ramona," said Mr. Quimby. "I didn't know. I am afraid you will have to do as the nurse says."

"Does she mean I'm *germy?*" Ramona was humiliated. "I took a shower this morning and washed my hands at the Whopperburger so I would be extra clean."

"Sometimes children are coming down with something and don't know it," explained Mr. Quimby. "Now, be a big girl and go downstairs and wait for us."

Ramona's eyes filled with tears of disappointment, but she found some pleasure in riding in the elevator alone. By the time she reached the lobby, she felt worse. The nurse called her a little girl. Her father called her a big girl. What was she? A germy girl.

Ramona sat gingerly on the edge of a Naugahyde couch. If she leaned back, she might get germs on it, or it might get germs on her. She swallowed hard. Was her throat a little bit sore? She thought maybe it was, way down in back. She put her hand to her forehead the way her mother did when she thought Ramona might have a fever. Her forehead was warm, maybe too warm.

As Ramona waited, she began to itch the way she itched when she had chickenpox. Her head itched, her back itched, her legs itched. Ramona scratched. A woman sat down on the couch, looked at Ramona, got up, and moved to another couch.

Ramona felt worse. She itched more and scratched harder. She swallowed often to see how her sore throat was coming along. She peeked down the neck of her blouse to see if she might have a rash and was surprised that she did not. She sniffed from time to time to see if she had a runny nose.

Now Ramona was angry. It would serve
everybody right if she came down with
some horrible disease, right there in their
old hospital. That would show everybody
how germfree the place was. Ramona
squirmed and gave that hard-to-reach
place between her shoulder blades a good
hard scratch. Then she scratched her head
with both hands. People stopped to stare.

A man in a white coat, with a
stethoscope hanging out of his pocket,
came hurrying through the lobby, glanced
at Ramona, stopped, and took a good look
at her. "How do you feel?" he asked.

"Awful," she admitted. "A nurse said I was too germy to go see my mother and new sister, but I think I caught some disease right here."

"I see," said the doctor. "Open your mouth and say 'ah.'"

Ramona *ahhed* until she gagged.

"Mh-hm," murmured the doctor. He looked so serious Ramona was alarmed. Then he pulled out his stethoscope and listened to her front and back, thumping as he did so. What was he hearing? Was there something wrong with her insides? Why didn't her father come?

The doctor nodded as if his worst suspicions had been confirmed. "Just as I thought," he said, pulling out his prescription pad.

Medicine, ugh. Ramona's twitching stopped. Her nose and throat felt fine. "I feel much better," she assured the doctor as she eyed that prescription pad with distrust.

"An acute case of siblingitis. Not at all unusual around here, but it shouldn't last long." He tore off the prescription he had written, instructed Ramona to give it to her father, and hurried on down the hall.

Ramona could not remember the name of her illness. She tried to read the doctor's scribbly cursive writing, but she could not. She could only read neat cursive, the sort her teacher wrote on the blackboard.

Itching again, she was still staring at the slip of paper when Mr. Quimby and Beezus stepped out of the elevator. "Roberta is so tiny." Beezus was radiant with joy. "And she is perfectly darling. She has a little round nose and—oh, when you see her, you'll love her."

"I'm sick." Ramona tried to sound pitiful. "I've got something awful. A doctor said so."

Beezus paid no attention. "And Roberta has brown hair—"

Mr. Quimby interrupted. "What's this all about, Ramona?"

"A doctor said I had something, some kind of *itis,* and I have to have this right away." She handed her father her prescription and scratched one shoulder. "If I don't, I might get sicker."

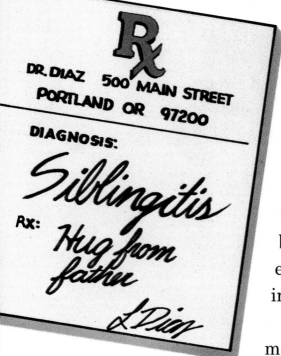

Mr. Quimby read the scribbly cursive, and then he did a strange thing. He lifted Ramona and gave her a big hug and a kiss, right there in the lobby. The itching stopped. Ramona felt much better. "You have acute siblingitis," explained her father. "*Itis* means inflammation."

Ramona already knew the meaning of sibling. Since her father had studied to be a teacher, brothers and sisters had become siblings to him.

"He understood you were worried and angry because you weren't allowed to see your new sibling, and prescribed attention," explained Mr. Quimby. "Now let's all go buy ice-cream cones before I fall asleep standing up."

Beezus said Roberta was too darling to be called a dumb word like sibling. Ramona felt silly, but she also felt better.

For the next three nights, Ramona took a book to the hospital and sat in the lobby, not reading, but sulking about the injustice of having to wait to see the strange new Roberta.

On the fourth day, Mr. Quimby took an hour off from the Shop-rite Market, picked up Beezus and Ramona, who were waiting in clean clothes, and drove to the hospital to bring home his wife and new daughter.

Ramona moved closer to Beezus when she saw her mother, holding a pink bundle, emerge from the elevator in a wheelchair pushed by a nurse and followed by Mr. Quimby carrying her bag. "Can't Mother walk?" she whispered.

"Of course she can walk," answered Beezus. "The hospital wants to make sure people get out without falling down and suing for a million dollars."

Mrs. Quimby waved to the girls. Roberta's face was hidden by a corner of a pink blanket, but the nurse had no time for a little girl eager to see a new baby. She pushed the wheelchair through the automatic door to the waiting car.

"*Now* can I see her?" begged Ramona when her

mother and Roberta were settled in the front, and the girls had climbed into the backseat.

"Dear Heart, of course you may." Mrs. Quimby then spoke the most beautiful words Ramona had ever heard, "Oh, Ramona, how I've missed you," as she turned back the blanket.

Ramona, leaning over the front seat for her first glimpse of the new baby sister, tried to hold her breath so she wouldn't breathe germs on Roberta, who did not look at all like the picture on the cover of *A Name for Your Baby*. Her face was bright pink, almost red, and her hair, unlike the smooth pale hair of the baby on the cover of the pamphlet, was dark and wild. Ramona did not know what to say. She did not feel that words like darling or adorable fitted this baby.

"She looks exactly like you looked when you were born," Mrs. Quimby told Ramona.

"She does?" Ramona found this hard to believe. She could not imagine that she had once looked like this red, frowning little creature.

"Well, what do you think of your new sister?" asked Mr. Quimby.

"She's so—so *little*," Ramona answered truthfully. Roberta opened her blue gray eyes.

"Mother!" cried Ramona. "She's cross-eyed."

Mrs. Quimby laughed. "All babies look cross-eyed sometimes. They outgrow it when they learn to focus." Sure enough, Roberta's eyes straightened out for a moment and then crossed again. She worked her mouth as if she didn't know what to do with it. She made little snuffling noises and lifted one arm as if she didn't know what it was for.

"Why does her nightie have those little pockets at the ends of the sleeves?" asked Ramona. "They cover up her hands."

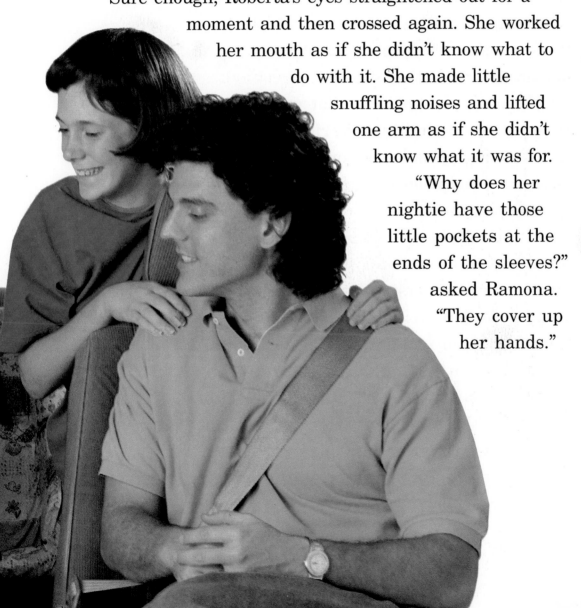

"They keep her from scratching herself," explained Mrs. Quimby. "She's too little to understand that fingernails scratch."

Ramona sat back and buckled her seat belt. She had once looked like Roberta. Amazing! She had once been that tiny, but she had grown, her hair had calmed down when she remembered to comb it, and she had learned to use her eyes and hands. "You know what I think?" she asked and did not wait for an answer. "I think it is hard work to be a baby." Ramona spoke as if she had discovered something unknown to the rest of the world. With her words came unexpected love and sympathy for the tiny person in her mother's arms.

"I hadn't thought of it that way," said Mrs. Quimby, "but I think you're right."

"Growing up is hard work," said Mr. Quimby as he drove away from the hospital. "Sometimes being grown-up is hard work."

"I know," said Ramona and thought some more. She thought about loose teeth, real sore throats, quarrels, misunderstandings with her teachers, longing for a bicycle her family could not afford, worrying when her parents bickered, how terrible she had felt when she hurt Beezus's feelings without meaning to, and all the long afternoons when Mrs. Kemp looked after her until her mother came from work. She had survived it all. "Isn't it funny?" she remarked as her father steered the car into their driveway.

"Isn't what funny?" asked her mother.

"That I used to be little and funny-looking and cross-eyed like Roberta," said Ramona. "And now look at me. I'm wonderful me!"

"Except when you're blunderful you," said Beezus.

Ramona did not mind when her family, except Roberta, who was too little, laughed. "Yup, wonderful, blunderful me," she said and was happy. She was winning at growing up.

# MEET
# BEVERLY CLEARY

In a tiny library, a small girl sat on a shabby leather chair and learned something amazing. "I made the most magic of discoveries. There were books for children!" she remembers. Soon after, that girl, Beverly Cleary, was reading all the children's books she could find.

Beverly Cleary didn't like every book she read. She found that some books were boring. She thought, "Why couldn't authors skip all that tiresome description and write books in which something happened on every page?"

When she was in the third grade, her school librarian gave her an idea. She could write books herself! Beverly Cleary recalls, "I wanted to read funny stories about the sort of children I knew and I decided that someday when I grew up I would write them."

Her chance came when she married and moved into a new house. In a closet, Cleary found stacks of typing paper. "Now I'll have to write a book," she told her husband. She began a story about a boy and a dog on a bus.

Children all over the world now know about Henry Huggins and his dog, Ribsy. They also know and love Ramona Quimby, who appears in a series of eight books. Two of these books, *Ramona Quimby, Age 8* and *Ramona and Her Father,* have been named Newbery Honor Books. Among Beverly Cleary's many other popular titles are *Henry and Beezus, The Mouse and the Motorcycle,* and *Ralph S. Mouse.*

# Don't Make At All

My mom says I'm her sugarplum.

My mom says I'm her lamb.

My mom says I'm completely perfect

Just the way I am.

My mom says I'm a super-special wonderful terrific

little guy.

My mom just had another baby.

Why?

Judith Viorst

# On GRANDDADDY'S Farm

## by Thomas B. Allen

*For Louise "Priss" McCallum*
*and*
*Dr. Benjamin Allen Shelton*
*In fond memory of*
*Granny and Granddaddy*

Over a bridge and down a tree-lined lane was Granddaddy's farm. It was there, in the rolling hills of middle Tennessee, that my cousins Priss and Ben Allen and I spent the summers.

Granddaddy was a brakeman for the L&N railroad and rode in the red caboose at the end of a long freight train. He worked the Nashville to Montgomery run and was away four days at a time.

Before he left the farm, he made sure that we three cousins knew what chores needed to be done while he was gone. We pumped water for the animals and weeded the vegetable garden. We fetched coal from the coal shed for Granny's stove and hauled water to the house from the dug well. Once we were entrusted with the job of hitching Old Mary, the big white draft horse, to the turning plow to cut a firebreak around the barn. A dry spell had left the ground so hard that one of us had to ride the plow to make it dig down into the packed earth.

Our little granny put in a full day baking and cooking, doing the wash, and taking care of the chickens and the garden. She also made sure that we cousins were well fed and well behaved and got our chores done.

After chores there was time for fun. One day Ben Allen dared me onto a yearling mule that had never had anything on his back before. When that mule felt me there, he started bucking and running around like crazy. I whooped and hollered like a rodeo rider as I hung on to his mane, while Priss and Ben Allen laughed till they cried. Granny, hearing the ruckus, came rushing out of the house. "Tom Burt, you get off that mule right now!" she yelled. The little mule gave one enormous buck and flipped me right into a thornbush.

The railroad yards weren't far from the farm, and
when Granddaddy's train came through the cut, headed
for home, the engineer gave a long pull on the whistle
cord, followed by three shorts, to let the families know
they were back. We knew it wouldn't be long before
Granddaddy would be coming down the lane, his empty
dinner basket riding lightly on his arm.

My cousins and I ran to meet him at the gate.
Granny stood on the front porch, smiling and wiping

her hands on her apron as if to say, "Yes, we're still here and everything's just fine."

After supper Granny and Granddaddy settled into their rockers on the porch to talk and enjoy the soft summer evening. Priss, Ben Allen, and I played outside till dark, shooting a scuffed-up basketball at the peach basket nailed above the car-shed door. We hoped Granny wouldn't tell about the yearling mule or any other trouble we'd gotten into.

We woke up every morning before dawn to the smell of biscuits baking and bacon frying. After a big breakfast we'd report to Granddaddy to get the day's assignment. I liked it best when it was a big job that needed doing, like bringing in the hay. It seemed more important than just doing chores.

After the hay was mowed and raked into windrows, we cousins piled it into stacks that Granddaddy tossed onto the wagon with one swoop of his pitchfork. It was hot work. Granny made several trips to the fields with a bucket of cool well water to quench our thirst. She always had something kind to say about our good work.

But for Priss, Ben Allen, and me the best part came after the hay was baled and stacked in the hayloft. We built a tunnel with the hay bales that we crawled through and then jumped from the loft into the straw piled below, again and again. We got covered with hay dust inside and out, but we did it anyway. The fun was worth the itching and sneezing.

Then Granny gave us a bar of fresh-smelling homemade soap to take down to the "blue hole" in Mill Creek. We hung our clothes on a tree limb and swam the dirt and dust away.

Sunday was the one day of the week when no work was done on Granddaddy's farm. After church more cousins and aunts and uncles came for Sunday dinner. All the cousins played baseball before dinner and took turns cranking the ice cream freezer. No matter how much ham and chicken and beans and potatoes and biscuits and tomatoes we ate, there was always room for homemade ice cream and Aunt Ruth's angel food cake.

Late in the afternoon the aunts and uncles and all the other cousins said their good-byes and drove off with everybody waving until the cars were out of sight. Half filled with excitement but half empty too, Priss, Ben Allen, and I looked for something to do to help level out those feelings. We went out behind the smokehouse to the horseshoe pits, where the uncles had just been, and pitched the rusty horseshoes that had once belonged to Old Mary.

Granddaddy liked to attend
the Sunday evening church
service, too, and he always invited
us cousins to go with him. We
hitched Old Mary to the buggy,
and with a "come up" and a light
slap of the reins, we were off at a
trot. The church was small and
plain. The benches were hard and
had no backs. Granddaddy sat
like a rock, listening to the words
of the preacher, while we shifted
and squirmed, trying to get
comfortable. We were sound
asleep by the time Old Mary
trotted us back through the gate
and up to the buggy shed.

It seemed like Granddaddy
had just come home when he had
to leave again for his run to
Montgomery. Granny filled his
basket with food for the journey.
It was all homegrown or homemade: smoked ham, put-up
vegetables, fresh fruit, biscuits,
butter, blackberry jam, cake and
pies. The basket weighed heavily
on his arm as he told us cousins
what chores needed to be done
and reminded us to take care of
Granny and the farm.

When we heard the train whistle blow, we knew that Granddaddy had swung up onto the steps of his <u>caboose</u>. We could hear the train move out of the yards and through the cut, the choo-choo-choo of the steam engine and the click-clack, clickety-clack of the rails quickening and blending into the steady rhythm that was the heartbeat of Granddaddy's life on the railroad.

The sound of the train became more and more distant and, no matter how hard we listened, was gone. The empty silence that followed was slowly filled with the distant "bobwhite" call of quail, the buzzing of insects, and the clucking of chickens. Priss, Ben Allen, and I got right to our chores. There was water to be pumped, animals to be tended. We were proud to be taking care of Granddaddy's farm.

# Meet
# Thomas B. Allen

In *On Granddaddy's Farm,* Thomas B. Allen tells about the wonderful summers he spent with his cousins on his grandfather's farm in Tennessee. "The 1930s were simpler times, hard times," he says. "I wanted to show that, regardless of the lack of 'things,' children had fun and did their chores to help out, too."

Allen tells children who want to be writers, "Write about things you know about, are interested in, and . . . have experienced. Write with your own voice." In writing *On Granddaddy's Farm,* Allen followed his own advice.

Allen has illustrated many award-winning books by other writers, including *Blackberries in the Dark* and *In Coal Country,* but writing and illustrating his own story was a very special experience.

Aunt Molly, two cousins, my brother Jimmy, and me on the farm, 1930s

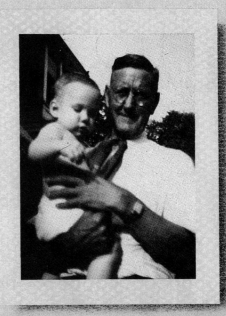

Granddaddy and me, 1929

In my studio in Carmel, New York, 1960s

My brother Jimmy (on the right) and me on the farm, 1930s

# Under the Sunday Tree

They walk together

on Sundays

move slowly

through the park

always remembering

to stop awhile

at the place where

two trees arch as one

leaves touching

like family

*Eloise Greenfield*

*Mr. Amos Ferguson's brightly colored folk-art painting shows a family group in the Bahamas. Eloise Greenfield wrote "Under the Sunday Tree" to go with Mr. Ferguson's painting.*

# INFORMATION ILLUSTRATED

Your guide to a world of information — with examples related to the themes you are exploring!

# CONTENTS

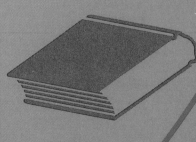

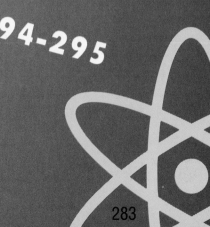

# BOOK PARTS

## SCIENCE AND YOU

By John M. Riley
Illustrated by
Marian Whalen

BETA PRESS • BOSTON

**TITLE PAGE**

## Contents

**TABLE OF CONTENTS**

# INDEX

## SEPARATION OF WHITE LIGHT INTO COLORS BY A PRISM

**A ray of white light is separated into seven colors when it passes through a prism:**

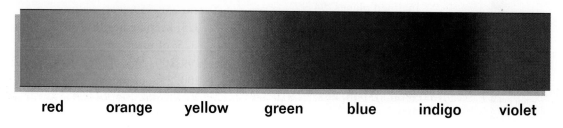

red    orange    yellow    green    blue    indigo    violet

## HOW IT WORKS

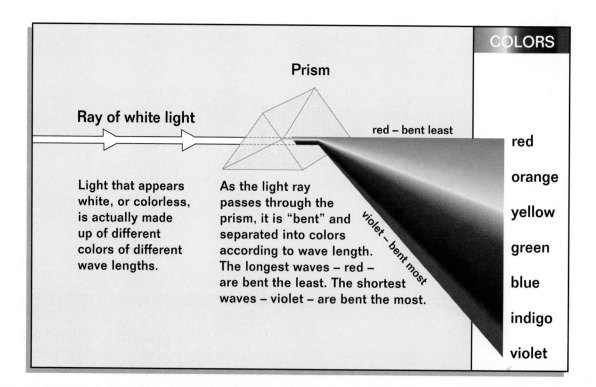

Prism

Ray of white light

red – bent least

violet – bent most

Light that appears white, or colorless, is actually made up of different colors of different wave lengths.

As the light ray passes through the prism, it is "bent" and separated into colors according to wave length. The longest waves – red – are bent the least. The shortest waves – violet – are bent the most.

COLORS

red

orange

yellow

green

blue

indigo

violet

# HOW WE SEE

## THE HUMAN EYE

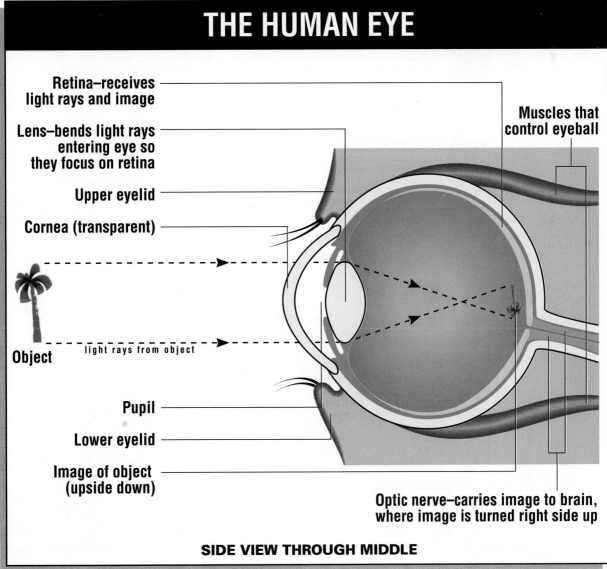

**Retina–receives light rays and image**

**Lens–bends light rays entering eye so they focus on retina**

**Upper eyelid**

**Cornea (transparent)**

**Muscles that control eyeball**

Object

light rays from object

**Pupil**

**Lower eyelid**

**Image of object (upside down)**

**Optic nerve–carries image to brain, where image is turned right side up**

**SIDE VIEW THROUGH MIDDLE**

287

# Dictionary

|  | |
|---|---|
| main entry | |
| definition | |
| syllable division | |
| pronunciation | |
| part of speech | |
| example sentence | |
| homographs | |

**moisten** To make or become slightly wet. I *moistened* the soil around the plant.
**moist·en** (moi′sən) *verb,* **moistened, moistening.**

**moisture** Water or other liquid in the air or on a surface; slight wetness. There was *moisture* on the window from the steam in the kitchen.
**mois·ture** (mois′chər) *noun.*

**molar** Any one of the large teeth at the back of the mouth. Molars have broad surfaces for grinding food.
**mo·lar** (mō′lər) *noun, plural* **molars.**

**molasses** A sweet, thick, yellowish brown syrup that is made from sugarcane.
**mo·las·ses** (mə las′iz) *noun.*

**mold¹** A hollow form that is made in a special shape. A liquid or soft material is poured into a mold. When it hardens, it takes the shape of the mold. *Noun.*
—**1.** To make into a special shape; form. We *molded* the clay with our hands. **2.** To influence and give form to. Our parents help *mold* our habits. *Verb.*
**mold** (mōld) *noun, plural* **molds;** *verb,* **molded, molding.**

**mold²** A furry-looking covering of fungus that grows on food and damp surfaces. *Noun.*
—To become covered with mold. The bread *molded* because it wasn't refrigerated. *Verb.*
**mold** (mōld) *noun, plural* **molds;** *verb,* **molded, molding.**

**molding** A strip of wood, plaster, or other material that is used along the edges of walls, windows, or doorways for decoration.
**mold·ing** (mōl′ding) *noun, plural* **moldings.**

**mole¹** A small, often raised, brown spot on the skin.
**mole** (mōl) *noun, plural* **moles.**

**mole²** A small animal with very soft, grayish fur that burrows holes underground. Moles have long claws and very small eyes.
**mole** (mōl) *noun, plural* **moles.**

**mole²**

**molecule** The smallest particle into which a substance can be divided without being changed chemically. For example, a molecule of water has two atoms of hydrogen and one atom of oxygen.
**mol·e·cule** (mol′ə kūl′) *noun, plural* **molecules.**

**mollusk** Any of a group of animals without backbones that usually have a soft body protected by a hard shell. Mollusks often live in or near water. Clams, snails, and oysters are mollusks.
**mol·lusk** (mol′əsk) *noun, plural* **mollusks.**

**molt** To shed the hair, feathers, skin, or shell and grow a new covering. Birds and snakes molt.
**molt** (mōlt) *verb,* **molted, molting.**

**molten** Melted by heat. Lava from a volcano is *molten* rock.
**mol·ten** (mōl′tən) *adjective.*

**mom** Mother. I call my mother *Mom.*
**mom** (mom) *noun, plural* **moms.**

**moment** **1.** A short period of time. I'll answer your question in just a *moment.* **2.** A particular point in time. Please come home the *moment* I call you or your dinner will get cold.
**mo·ment** (mō′mənt) *noun, plural* **moments.**

**momentary** Lasting only a short time. There was a *momentary* lull in the storm and then it rained heavily again.
**mo·men·tar·y** (mō′mən ter′ē) *adjective.*

**momentous** Having great importance. The end of the war was a *momentous* event for all.
**mo·men·tous** (mō men′təs) *adjective.*

**momentum** The force or speed that an object has when it is moving. A rock gains *momentum* as it rolls down a hill.
**mo·men·tum** (mō men′təm) *noun, plural* **momentums.**

**Mon.** An abbreviation for *Monday.*

**monarch** **1.** A king, queen, or other ruler of a state or country. **2.** A large orange and black butterfly found in North America.
**mon·arch** (mon′ərk) *noun, plural* **monarchs.**

**monarchy** **1.** Government by a king, queen, or other monarch. **2.** A nation or state that is ruled by a monarch.
**mon·ar·chy** (mon′ər kē) *noun, plural* **monarchies.**

**monastery** A place where monks live and work together.
**mon·as·ter·y** (mon′ə ster′ē) *noun, plural* **monasteries.**

472

word history

guide words

plural

illustration

compound word

verb forms

pronunciation key

---

**Monday** The second day of the week.
**Mon·day** (mun′dē *or* mun′dā) *noun, plural* **Mondays.**

### Word History

The Romans dedicated the second day of the week to the moon. This name was translated as an Old English word meaning "moon's day," or **Monday** as it became in modern English.

**monetary** Of, in, or having to do with money or currency. This vase has great *monetary* value. The dollar is the *monetary* unit of the United States.
**mon·e·tar·y** (mon′i ter′ē) *adjective.*

**money** The coins and paper currency of a country. Money is used to buy goods and pay people for services. Nickels, dimes, and dollar bills are money.
**mon·ey** (mun′ē) *noun, plural* **moneys.**

**Mongolia** A country in central Asia.
**Mon·go·li·a** (mong gō′lē ə) *noun.*

**mongoose** A slender animal that has a pointed face, a long tail, and rough, shaggy fur. Mongooses live in Africa and Asia. They eat rats and mice and are very quick.
**mon·goose** (mong′güs′) *noun, plural* **mongooses.**

mongoose

**mongrel** An animal, especially a dog, or a plant that is a mixture of breeds.
**mon·grel** (mung′grəl *or* mong′grəl) *noun, plural* **mongrels.**

**monitor** 1. A student who is given a special duty to do. Some monitors help take attendance and others help keep order. 2. Any person who warns or keeps watch. The sailor's job was to be *monitor* of the radar screen. 3. The screen that a computer uses to display numbers, letters, and pictures. It is similar to a television screen. *Noun.*
—To watch over or observe something. Our teacher *monitored* the fire drill. *Verb.*
**mon·i·tor** (mon′i tər) *noun, plural* **monitors;** *verb,* **monitored, monitoring.**

**monk** A man who has joined a religious order, lives in a monastery, and is bound by religious vows.
**monk** (mungk) *noun, plural* **monks.**

**monkey** 1. Any of a group of intelligent, furry animals with long tails and hands and feet that can grasp things. Most monkeys live in trees in tropical areas of the world. Monkeys are primates. 2. A playful or naughty child. *Noun.*
—To fool or play around in a mischievous way. The lifeguard asked us to quit *monkeying* around in the water. Don't *monkey* with the stove or you might get burned. *Verb.*
**mon·key** (mung′kē) *noun, plural* **monkeys;** *verb,* **monkeyed, monkeying.**

monkey

**monkey wrench** A wrench with a jaw that can be adjusted to fit different sizes of nuts and bolts.

**monogram** A design made by combining two or more initials of a person's name. You see monograms on such things as clothing, towels, and stationery.
**mon·o·gram** (mon′ə gram′) *noun, plural* **monograms.**

**monologue** 1. A long dramatic or comic speech or performance given by one person. The audience wept during the actor's *monologue* in the second act of the play. 2. A long speech made by one person who is part of a group.
**mon·o·logue** (mon′ə lôg′ *or* mon′ə log′) *noun, plural* **monologues.**

**monopolize** 1. To get or have a monopoly of. 2. To get, have, or use all of. Don't *monopolize* the teacher's attention.
**mo·nop·o·lize** (mə nop′ə līz′) *verb,* **monopolized, monopolizing.**

**monopoly** 1. The sole control of a product or service by a person or company. That bus

---

at; āpe; fär; câre; end; mē; it; ice; pîerce; hot; ōld; sông, fôrk; oil; out; up; ūse; rüle; pùll; tûrn; chin; sing; shop; thin; this; hw in white; zh in treasure. The symbol ə stands for the unstressed vowel sound in about, taken, pencil, lemon, and circus.

473

289

# Directions

## HOW TO STEP THROUGH A PIECE OF PAPER

### WHAT YOU WILL NEED:

a piece of typing paper (8 1/2 × 11 inches), a ruler, a pencil, a pair of scissors

### WHAT TO DO:

**1**
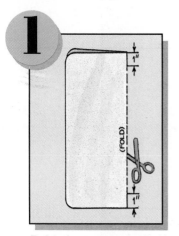
Fold the paper in half lengthwise, then cut along the fold to within 1 inch of each end.

**2**
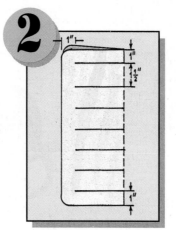
With the paper folded and the fold to the right, draw 7 straight lines from right to left across the paper, stopping 1 inch from the left side. Start 1 inch from the top of the paper, and make the lines 1 1/2 inches apart.

**3**
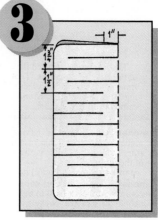
Now, starting 1 3/4 inches from the top of the paper, draw 6 straight lines from left to right across the paper, stopping 1 inch from the right side. Make the lines 1 1/2 inches apart.

**4**

Carefully cut along the lines you have drawn.

**5**
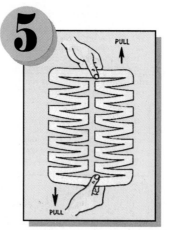
Unfold the paper and gently pull the ends apart.

**6**

The paper will open into a narrow band that you can easily step through.

290

# HOW TO SEND A SECRET MESSAGE TO A FRIEND

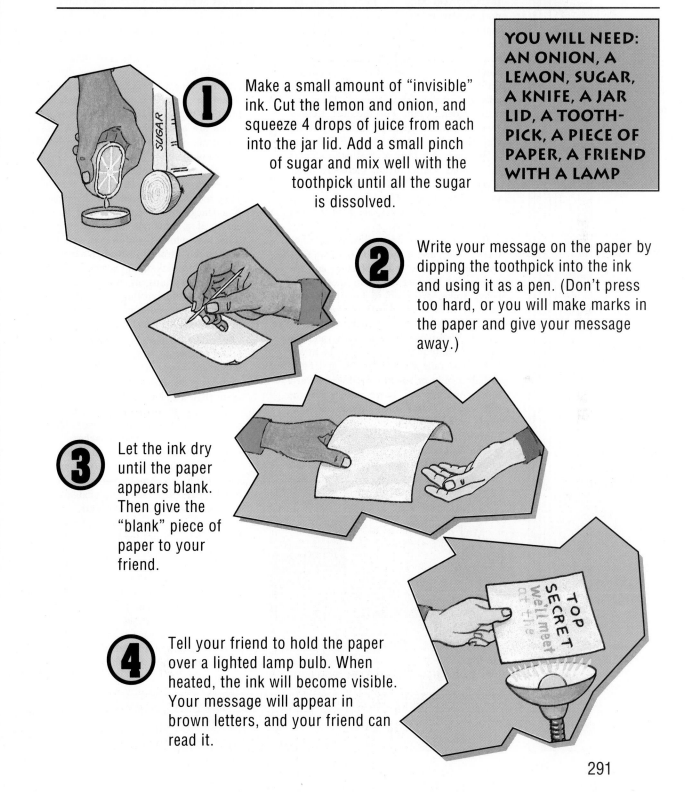

**YOU WILL NEED: AN ONION, A LEMON, SUGAR, A KNIFE, A JAR LID, A TOOTH-PICK, A PIECE OF PAPER, A FRIEND WITH A LAMP**

**1** Make a small amount of "invisible" ink. Cut the lemon and onion, and squeeze 4 drops of juice from each into the jar lid. Add a small pinch of sugar and mix well with the toothpick until all the sugar is dissolved.

**2** Write your message on the paper by dipping the toothpick into the ink and using it as a pen. (Don't press too hard, or you will make marks in the paper and give your message away.)

**3** Let the ink dry until the paper appears blank. Then give the "blank" piece of paper to your friend.

**4** Tell your friend to hold the paper over a lighted lamp bulb. When heated, the ink will become visible. Your message will appear in brown letters, and your friend can read it.

entry word

**RAILROADS** May 10, 1869, was an important day in the history of the United States. On that day a spike was driven that joined a railroad being built westward from Omaha, Neb., with a railroad being built eastward from Sacramento, Calif. The two roads were the Union Pacific and the Central Pacific. They met near Ogden, Utah. For the first time it was possible to travel by railroad all the way across the country.

Railroads now form a great network over the United States. In all, there are about 225,000 miles of them—just about enough to go to the moon. The country's railroads have had a great deal to do with building it into a strong nation.

It is easy to see how railroads got their name. They are truly roads built of rails. Standard rails are made of steel and are in sections 39 feet long. In most tracks heavy spikes are used to fasten the rails securely to wooden crossties. The ties are laid on beds of crushed rock, cinders, or gravel. Water can run off easily, and the ties stay firmly in place. Some of the newer tracks use rails welded into long lengths of half a mile or so—in some cases several miles. Another way newer tracks may be different is in the ties. Instead of being made of wood, they may be concrete. In Europe many tracks have steel ties.

The distance of the two rails from each other in a railroad track is called the gauge. Standard gauge is 4 feet, 8½ inches. Most tracks in the United States are built on this gauge. It is possible for cars and engines of one railroad company to run on the tracks of other companies.

Many railroad tracks are double. One track is for trains going in one direction, and the other is for trains going in the other direction. If there is only one track, there must be sidings every so often. When two trains are approaching each other, one of the trains pulls off on a siding to let the other one pass.

Railroad companies build their tracks as nearly level and straight as they can. They avoid sharp corners and steep slopes. If a track must bend, it is laid in a big curve. If a mountain is in the way, the track may wind up and over it, or a tunnel may be dug through it. Bridges carry tracks over swamps, lakes, and rivers.

Passenger trains are not as common as they once were, but they are still an important way of carrying people from place to place. More than 300 million passengers a year ride on passenger trains in the United States. Carrying freight is an even more important work of railroads. The freight carried by American railroads amounts to more than a billion tons a year.

To carry their passengers and freight, railroads use many kinds of cars. On passenger trains we find coaches; diners; sleepers of several kinds; observation, or lounge, cars; and baggage cars. Some lines have dome cars. Among the many kinds of freight cars are tank cars, flatcars, boxcars, stockcars, refrigerator cars, and gondolas and hopper cars. Many freight cars have special fittings for carrying a particular kind of goods.

Much freight today travels piggyback on flatcars. Loaded truck trailers are put on the flatcars and then taken off the cars at the right city. The freight can be truck delivered at the exact spot where it is wanted. Another way freight is now handled is in containers of a standard size for travel by air, truck, ship, or train. The containers

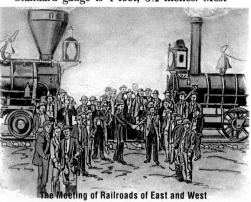
The Meeting of Railroads of East and West

are quickly and easily transferred from one travel system to another.

Locomotives of different kinds pull the trains. Most of them are diesel-electric locomotives. Others are electric. Once steam locomotives were common, but over most of the world steam is no longer used.

It takes more than half a million people in the United States to keep the country's railroads running. In addition to the train crews themselves, there must be many workers in the railway yards, the repair shops, and the railway stations.

With so many trains on the railroads, there must be good signal systems to prevent wrecks and keep the trains on schedule. Many different ways of signaling are in use. They range from long-established ways such as semaphores and colored lights to completely automatic electronic control systems. In some cases no crew is needed.

One of the most remarkable things about railroads is how fast they developed. One does not have to go very far back beyond the day the two roads met in Utah to find the very beginning of railroads. Their ancestors were roads of wooden rails over which, in the early 1600's, horses pulled coal cars away from English coal mines. But the modern railroad goes back only to 1825, when the Stockton and Darlington Railway was built in England. The first American railroad built for carrying both freight and passengers was the Baltimore and Ohio. It was started in 1827, but not till several years later did good steam locomotives make regular service satisfactory. How strange a train of those days, with its passenger cars like stagecoaches, would look beside a modern train!

Though railroads are not as important as they were before the days of automobiles, buses, trucks, and airplanes, they are still often the best way of moving things on land. Trains can travel in almost any kind of weather and carry any kind of goods. (See BRIDGES; LOCOMOTIVE; SUBWAY; SIGNALING; TUNNELS.)

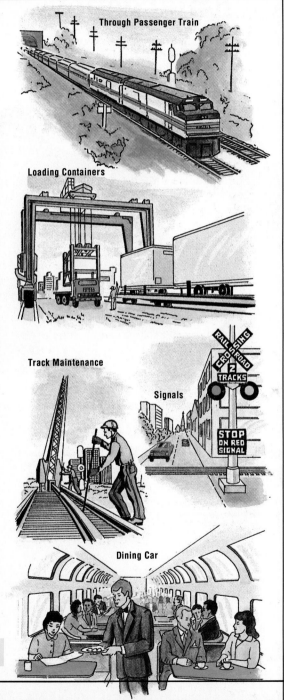

Through Passenger Train

Loading Containers

Track Maintenance

Signals

RAILROAD CROSSING
2 TRACKS

STOP ON RED SIGNAL

Dining Car

# For Emergency Calls Only

# 9-1-1

**LISTINGS FOR EMERGENCY AGENCIES ARE CONTINUED ON PAGE A2**

**Fire and Rescue**

**Police Sheriff Highway Patrol**

**Ambulance**

**Coast Guard Search and Rescue**

**For Non-Emergency Calls please use the appropriate 7-digit number.**

Telephone numbers for City, County, State, and Federal agencies are listed in the White Pages.

Write in local number here:

Doctor _____

**Telecommunications Device for the Deaf (TDD) Emergency Calls:**

*Dial 9-1-1

*Press the Space Bar Until Someone Answers.

En una emergencia la forma más rápida de obtener auxilio es marcar 9-1-1

**Notice!**

**Dialing 9-1-1 and Your Privacy**
When reporting an emergency by dialing 9-1-1, your number (including non-published number) and address may be automatically displayed on a viewing screen. This information enables the emergency agency to quickly locate you if the call is interrupted.

If you do not wish to have your telephone number and address displayed, use the appropriate 7-digit emergency number.

# EMERGENCY NUMBERS

## 128 PHOTO—POLLARD

| | |
|---|---|
| Photo Phinishers 12 Beltway......................555-4235 | Pittman Gale 64 River St.....................555-9978 |
| Phung Yan Chu 16 Center Ave.....................555-0971 | Pittman Roger MD |
| **PHYLLIS'S PET SHOP** |     1245 Santa Ana Blvd.................555-9863 |
|     1166 Park Hwy.............**555-8920** | Pitts Loleta 133 Allen Way ..........................555-8359 |
| Pichard Nell 18 Dysart Ave ......................555-9810 | Pizel John 501 Whitney Ave ........................555-8252 |
| Pichard Roberto 9 Day St .........................555-9356 | **PLAINVILLE BOAT SHOP** |
| Pickett Ana 809 Buena Vista .......................555-0842 |     1621 Park Hwy.....................**555-2769** |
| Picovsky Susan 62 Wood St .....................555-9854 | Plante Kevan 113 River St.............555-7458 |
| Pidgeon C G 920 Main St .........................555-4845 | Plante Sylvia 113 River St.............555-7460 |
| Pie & Cake Co 622 Park Hwy .......................555-7590 | Pletcher Arlen 75 Wood St .......................555-3148 |
| Piedra Bill 51 Horace St............................555-8592 | Plumisto LeRoy 441 River St .....................555-2323 |
| Piedras M................Dysart Ave .........555-4521 | ...a 2 Allen Way............692... |

## WHITE PAGES

# GLOS

This glossary can help you to pronounce and find out the meanings of words in this book that you may not know.

The words are listed in alphabetical order. Guide words at the top of each page tell you the first and last words on the page.

Each word is divided into syllables. The way to pronounce each word is given next. You will be able to understand the pronunciation respelling by using the key to the right. A shorter key appears at the bottom right corner of every other page.

When a word has more than one syllable, a dark accent mark (´) shows which syllable is stressed. In some words, a light accent mark (´) shows which syllable has a less heavy stress.

Glossary entries are based on entries in *The Macmillan/McGraw-Hill School Dictionary 1.*

| | | | |
|---|---|---|---|
| a | at, bad | d | dear, soda, bad |
| ā | ape, pain, day, break | f | five, defend, leaf, off, cough, elephant |
| ä | father, car, heart | g | game, ago, fog, egg |
| âr | care, pair, bear, their, where | h | hat, ahead |
| e | end, pet, said, heaven, friend | hw | white, whether, which |
| ē | equal, me, feet, team, piece, key | j | joke, enjoy, gem, page, edge |
| i | it, big, English, hymn | k | kite, bakery, seek, tack, cat |
| ī | ice, fine, lie, my | l | lid, sailor, feel, ball, allow |
| îr | ear, deer, here, pierce | m | man, family, dream |
| o | odd, hot, watch | n | not, final, pan, knife |
| ō | old, oat, toe, low | ng | long, singer, pink |
| ô | coffee, all, taught, law, fought | p | pail, repair, soap, happy |
| ôr | order, fork, horse, story, pour | r | ride, parent, wear, more, marry |
| oi | oil, toy | s | sit, aside, pets, cent, pass |
| ou | out, now | sh | shoe, washer, fish, mission, nation |
| u | up, mud, love, double | t | tag, pretend, fat, button, dressed |
| ū | use, mule, cue, feud, few | th | thin, panther, both |
| ü | rule, true, food | <u>th</u> | this, mother, smooth |
| u̇ | put, wood, should | v | very, favor, wave |
| ûr | burn, hurry, term, bird, word, courage | w | wet, weather, reward |
| ə | about, taken, pencil, lemon, circus | y | yes, onion |
| b | bat, above, job | z | zoo, lazy, jazz, rose, dogs, houses |
| ch | chin, such, match | zh | vision, treasure, seizure |

297

**absent-mindedly** Not paying attention to what is going on. The child stared out the window *absent-mindedly*.
    **ab•sent-mind•ed•ly** (ab´sənt mīn´did lē) *adverb*.

**acrobatic** **1.** Changing position quickly. **2.** Relating to a person who is skilled at performing stunts such as walking on a tightrope or swinging on a trapeze. The circus performer made an *acrobatic* leap.
    **ac•ro•bat•ic** (ak´rə bat´ik) *adjective*.

**acute** **1.** Developing suddenly and becoming severe. I got an *acute* pain in my side from running too far. **2.** Very keen or quick. My vision became *acute* when I started wearing glasses.
    **a•cute** (ə kūt´) *adjective*.

**Aiko** (ä ē´ kō)

**Algie** (al´jē)

**amid** In the middle of. The house stood *amid* a grove of pine trees.
    **a•mid** (ə mid´) *preposition*.

**angle** The figure formed by two lines or flat surfaces that stretch out from one point or line.
    **an•gle** (ang´gəl) *noun*.

*acrobatic*

*antenna*

**antenna** One of a pair of long, thin body parts, such as that on the head of an insect or a lobster; feeler. Antennae are used to sense touch and smells.
   **an•ten•na** (an ten´ə) *noun, plural* **antennae** (an ten´ē).

**anxiously** In a nervous, worried, or fearful way. My cousin *anxiously* gripped the steering wheel as he drove on the slippery mountain roads.
   **anx•ious•ly** (angk´shəs lē) *adverb*.

**application** 1. Something that is put on, such as an ointment. This *application* will soothe your bruise. 2. The act of putting something to use. The *application* of scientific knowledge has made space exploration possible. 3. A written form used in making a request. I filled out the *application* for the job.
   **ap•pli•ca•tion** (ap´li kā´shən) *noun*.

**arch¹** To form a curve. The stone bridge *arched* over the river.
   **arch** (ärch) *verb*, **arched, arching**.

**arch²** Sly and playful. She teased me with an *arch* smile on her face.
   **arch** (ärch) *adjective*.

**astonishing** Causing great surprise; amazing. The news that I had won the contest was *astonishing*.
   **as•ton•ish•ing** (ə ston´ə shing) *adjective*.

**awl** A pointed tool used for making small holes in leather or wood.
▲ Another word that sounds like this is **all**.
   **awl** (ôl) *noun*.

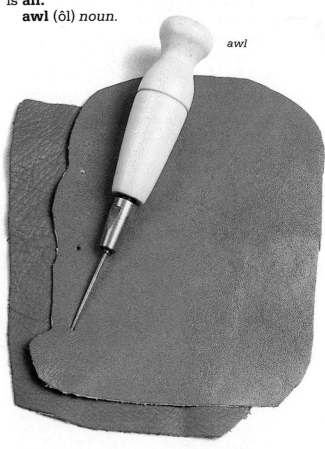

*awl*

---

**Word History**

The word **arch** comes from the Latin word *arcus,* which means "bow," a weapon made with a curved piece of wood that is used to shoot arrows.

---

at; āpe; fär; câre; end; mē; it; īce; pîerce; hot; ōld; sông; fôrk; oil; out; up; ūse; rüle; pu̇ll; tûrn; chin; sing; shop; thin; <u>th</u>is; hw in **wh**ite; zh in treasure. The symbol ə stands for the unstressed vowel sound in about, taken, pencil, lemon, and circus.

# B

**bale** To make into a bundle. The workers *baled* the cotton.
**bale** (bāl) *verb*, **baled, baling.**

**barb** A sharp point that sticks out backward or at an angle from something else. The *barb* of the fishhook caught in the fish's mouth.
**barb** (bärb) *noun*.

**barrigón** Spanish for "potbellied."
**ba•rri•gón** (bä rē gōn´) *adjective*.

**bassinette** Another spelling of **bassinet.** A basketlike bed for a baby, often with a hood at one end.
**bas•si•nette** (bas´ə net´) *noun*.

**bicker** To quarrel in a noisy way about something that is not very important. The two brothers *bickered* over whose turn it was to mow the lawn.
**bick•er** (bik´ər) *verb*, **bickered, bickering.**

**bicuspid** A tooth with two points. A grown person has eight bicuspids.
**bi•cus•pid** (bī kus´pid) *noun*.

---

### Word History
The word **bicuspid** comes from *bi-*, a Latin word beginning that means "two," and the Latin word *cuspis*, meaning "point."

---

**bitter** Having a harsh, sharp, unpleasant taste. I did not like the *bitter* cough medicine.
**bit•ter** (bit´ər) *adjective*.

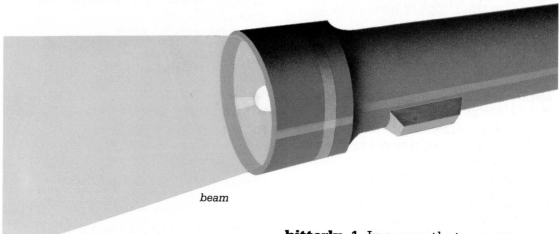

*beam*

**beam** A narrow ray of light. A *beam* of sunlight came through the window. The campers could see the path by the *beam* of the flashlight. *Noun.* —To smile happily. The parents *beamed* with pride as their child gave a speech. *Verb.*
**beam** (bēm) *noun; verb*, **beamed, beaming.**

**bitterly** **1.** In a way that causes or shows sorrow or pain. The child cried *bitterly* from the pain. **2.** In a way that shows anger, resentment, or hatred. The two rivals fought *bitterly* at times.
**bit•ter•ly** (bit´ər lē) *adverb*.

**blinding** Causing inability to see. The *blinding* light of the sun is too bright to look at for long.
**blind•ing** (blīn´ding) *adjective*.

*bouquet*

**bouquet** A bunch of flowers. I brought a *bouquet* of tulips to my sick friend.
    **bou•quet** (bō kā´ *or* bü kā´) *noun.*

**brakeman** A person who helps the conductor of a railroad train. In the past, the brakeman's job was to operate the train's brakes.
    **brake•man** (brāk´mən) *noun, plural* **brakemen.**

**brim** An edge or rim. My glass is filled to the *brim.* That beach hat has a wide *brim.*
    **brim** (brim) *noun.*

**brittle** Very easily broken. The *brittle* icicles snapped in two when I touched them.
    **brit•tle** (brit´əl) *adjective.*

**bronco** A small, partly wild horse of the western United States.
    **bron•co** (brong´kō) *noun.*

*bronco*

**buggy** A light carriage with four wheels. A buggy is pulled by one horse.
    **bug•gy** (bug´ē) *noun, plural* **buggies.**

**burner** The part of a stove from which the flame or heat comes. Put the pot on the back *burner* of the stove.
    **burn•er** (bûr´nər) *noun.*

# C

**cannery** A factory where food is canned. The men and women worked in a fruit *cannery.*
    **can•ner•y** (kan´ə rē) *noun, plural* **canneries.**

---

at; āpe; fär; câre; end; mē; it; īce; pîerce; hot; ōld; sông; fôrk; oil; out; up; ūse; rüle; pu̇ll; tûrn; chin; sing; shop; thin; this; hw in white; zh in treasure. The symbol ə stands for the unstressed vowel sound in about, taken, pencil, lemon, and circus.

---

**caress** To touch or stroke gently and with love; pet. The child *caressed* the kitten fondly.
  **ca•ress** (kə res´) *verb,* **caressed, caressing.**

**cattail** A tall plant with long, flat leaves that grows in marshes. Cattails have long, furry brown flower spikes.
  **cat•tail** (kat´tāl) *noun.*

**chamber** **1.** An enclosed space. The human heart has four *chambers.* **2.** A room in a house or other building.
  **cham•ber** (chām´ bər) *noun.*

**chopsticks** A pair of long, thin sticks that are used to eat with. Chopsticks are held between the thumb and fingers of one hand.
  **chop•sticks** (chop´stiks´) *plural noun.*

**chortle** To laugh with a snorting chuckle. The boy *chortled* when he thought about the clown.
  **chor•tle** (chôr´təl) *verb,* **chortled, chortling.**

**Chou** (jō)

*cattail*

**cellophane** A thin, clear material made from cellulose. Cellophane is used to wrap food and to make clear tape.
  **cel•lo•phane** (sel´ə fān´) *noun.*

**churn** To stir or move with a forceful motion. The boat's paddle *churned* the water. *Verb.* —A container in which cream or milk is shaken or beaten to make butter. *Noun.*
  **churn** (chûrn) *verb,* **churned, churning;** *noun.*

302

**clenched** Closed together tightly. His *clenched* fist showed that he was angry.
    **clenched** (klencht) *adjective.*

**collapsed** Fallen in; broken down or failed. The *collapsed* staircase made it impossible to reach the second floor.
    **col•lapsed** (kə lapst´) *adjective.*

**contagious** Able to be spread from person to person. Nearly everyone in the class caught chicken pox because it is so *contagious.*
    **con•ta•gious** (kən tā´jəs) *adjective.*

**coop** A cage or pen for chickens, rabbits, or other small animals. Our neighbor keeps chickens in a *coop* behind the house.
    **coop** (küp) *noun.*

*crystal*

**crystal** A body that is formed by certain substances when they change into a solid. Crystals have flat surfaces and a regular shape. Salt forms in crystals. Snowflakes are crystals.
    **crys•tal** (kris´təl) *noun.*

*coop*

at; āpe; fär; câre; end; mē; it; īce; pîerce; hot; ōld; sông; fôrk; oil; out; up; ūse; rüle; pull; tûrn; chin; sing; shop; thin; **th**is; hw in **wh**ite; **zh** in treasure. The symbol ə stands for the unstressed vowel sound in about, taken, pencil, lemon, and circus.

303

**cunning** Very clever at fooling or deceiving others; sly.
cun•ning (kun´ing) *adjective.*

**cursive** Written or printed with the letters joined together. She signed her name using *cursive* handwriting.
cur•sive (kûr´siv) *adjective.*

*cursive*

**cut** **1.** A path made by cutting, digging, or blasting. The crew worked all day digging the railroad *cut.* **2.** A decrease. The store announced a *cut* in its prices. *Noun.*
—**1.** To have a tooth or teeth grow through the gum. The baby *cut* a new tooth yesterday. **2.** To cross or pass. The river *cuts* through the valley. *Verb.*
cut (kut) *noun; verb,* **cut, cutting.**

# D

**dainty** Delicate and pretty. The fine handkerchief was decorated with a *dainty* design.
dain•ty (dān´tē) *adjective.*

**dangle** To hang or swing loosely. Some old kite string *dangled* from a branch of the tree.
dan•gle (dang´gəl) *verb,* **dangled, dangling.**

**deem** To think; believe; judge. Do you *deem* it wise to accept that job?
deem (dēm) *verb,* **deemed, deeming.**

**delicate** **1.** Finely skilled or sensitive. *Delicate* instruments detected an earthquake thousands of miles away. **2.** Fine or dainty. The threads of a spider's web are *delicate.*
del•i•cate (del´i kit) *adjective.*

**dentine** The hard, bony material that forms the main part of the tooth. It is covered by the enamel. Dentine is very sensitive to heat, cold, and touch.
den•tine (den tēn´) *noun.*

**depart** To go away; leave. The train is due to *depart* from the station at ten o'clock.
de•part (di pärt´) *verb,* **departed, departing.**

**dew** Moisture from the air that forms drops on cool surfaces. Dew gathers on grass, plants, and trees during the night. ▲ Other words that sound like this are **do** and **due.**
dew (dü *or* dū) *noun.*

*dew*

**diagonally** On a slant. The rope was tied *diagonally* across the window.
di•ag•o•nal•ly (dī ag´ə nə lē) *adverb.*

**dignity** The condition of being aware of one's honor and worthiness, as shown in a proud, calm appearance or manner. Despite great hardship and poverty, my grandparents kept their *dignity*.
  **dig•ni•ty** (dig′ni tē) *noun.*

**direct** With nothing in between. A kettle of water needs *direct* heat in order to come to a full boil. *Adjective.* —**1.** To manage or control. A police officer *directs* traffic at the busy intersection. **2.** To tell or show someone the way. Can you *direct* me to the nearest bus stop? *Verb.*
  **di•rect** (di rekt′ *or* dī rekt′) *adjective; verb,* **directed, directing.**

**disappointment** The feeling a person has when hopes are not met. Roberta couldn't hide her *disappointment* when it rained and the picnic was called off.
  **dis•ap•point•ment** (dis′ə point′mənt) *noun.*

**disc** Another spelling of **disk.** Look up **disk** for more information.

**disguise** To change the way one looks in order to hide one's real identity or look like someone else. The children *disguised* themselves as clowns, pirates, and monsters on Halloween.
  **dis•guise** (dis gīz′) *verb,* **disguised, disguising.**

**disk** A flat, thin, round object. This word is also spelled **disc.**
  **disk** (disk) *noun.*

**distance** The amount of space between two things or points. The *distance* from my house to the school is two blocks.
  **dis•tance** (dis′təns) *noun.*

**distant** Far away in space or time; not near. The novel told of a family that had traveled to the United States from a *distant* country.
  **dis•tant** (dis′tənt) *adjective.*

**distrust** A belief that someone or something is not honest or true; suspicion. The boy made so many false promises that his friends were filled with *distrust*.
  **dis•trust** (dis trust′) *noun.*

**disturb** **1.** To upset or change the order of things. The wind *disturbed* the papers on the table. **2.** To make uneasy or nervous; upset. Loud music *disturbs* my grandmother. The news of the accident *disturbed* us all.
  **dis•turb** (di stûrb′) *verb,* **disturbed, disturbing.**

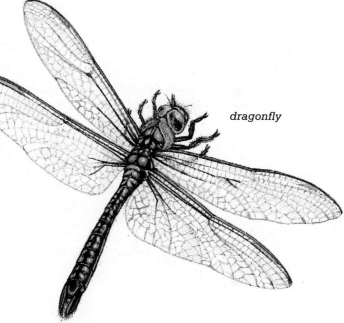

*dragonfly*

**dragonfly** An insect that has a long, thin body and two pairs of wings. Dragonflies eat mosquitoes and other insects. They live near fresh water.
  **drag•on•fly** (drag′ən flī′) *noun, plural* **dragonflies.**

at; āpe; fär; câre; end; mē; it; īce; pîerce; hot; ōld; sông; fôrk; oil; out; up; ūse; rüle; pùll; tûrn; chin; sing; shop; thin; this; hw in white; zh in treasure. The symbol ə stands for the unstressed vowel sound in about, taken, pencil, lemon, and circus.

**draught** Another spelling of **draft**. A current of air in an enclosed space. I could feel a cold *draught* from the open window.
**draught** (draft) *noun.*

*dusk*

**dusk** The time of day just before the sun goes down; twilight. The farmer worked in the fields from dawn to *dusk.*
**dusk** (dusk) *noun.*

**eager** Wanting very much to do something. A person who is eager is full of interest and enthusiasm. The children were *eager* to go to the circus.
**ea•ger** (ē′gər) *adjective.*

**eldest** Born first; oldest. I am the *eldest* of three children.
**eld•est** (el′dist) *adjective.*

**embrace** To take or hold in the arms as a sign of love or friendship; hug. The children *embraced* their parents as soon as they got off the plane.
**em•brace** (em brās′) *verb,*
**embraced, embracing.**

**emerge** To come into view. The sun *emerged* from behind a cloud.
**e•merge** (i mûrj′) *verb,* **emerged, emerging.**

**entrust** To put someone or something in the care of a person. We *entrusted* our neighbors with the care of our dog over the weekend.
**en•trust** (en trust′) *verb,* **entrusted, entrusting.**

**et cetera** Latin words that mean "and so forth" or "and others." We went to the store and bought milk, fish, vegetables, *et cetera.* Et cetera is usually abbreviated as **etc.**
**et cet•er•a** (et set′ə rə).

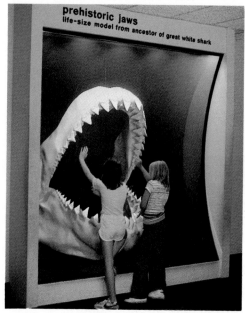
*exhibit*

**exhibit** Something shown. We went to see the *exhibit* of African art at the museum. The science *exhibit* won first prize.
**ex•hib•it** (eg zib′it) *noun.*

**expedition** A journey made for a particular reason. The scientists made an *expedition* to Alaska to study the animals in the area.
**ex•pe•di•tion** (ek′spi dish′ən) *noun.*

*extractor*

**extractor** A person or thing that pulls or gets something out. Miyo used a juice *extractor* to make orange juice.
**ex•trac•tor** (ek strak´tər) *noun.*

**fanciful** Imaginary; unreal. The storyteller told a *fanciful* tale about dragons.
**fan•ci•ful** (fan´sə fəl) *adjective.*

**feverish** Having a body temperature that is higher than normal. The child was so hot from playing in the sun that she seemed *feverish*.
**fe•ver•ish** (fē´vər ish) *adjective.*

**filament** A very fine thread or wire. In an electric light bulb, the filament is a fine wire that gives off light when an electric current passes through it.
**fil•a•ment** (fil´ə mənt) *noun.*

**firebreak** A strip of land that is plowed or cleared so that it will stop the spread of a fire.
**fire•break** (fīr´ brāk´) *noun.*

**fixture** Something that is firmly and permanently fastened into place. A bathtub, a toilet, and a sink are bathroom fixtures.
**fix•ture** (fiks´chər) *noun.*

**fleet¹** 1. A group of warships under one command. The admiral ordered the *fleet* to sail. 2. A group of ships, airplanes, or cars. My cousin owns a *fleet* of taxicabs.
**fleet** (flēt) *noun.*

at; āpe; fär; câre; end; mē; it; īce; pîerce; hot; ōld; sông; fôrk; oil; out; up; ūse; rüle; pu̇ll; tûrn; chin; sing; shop; thin; this; hw in white; zh in treasure. The symbol ə stands for the unstressed vowel sound in about, taken, pencil, lemon, and circus.

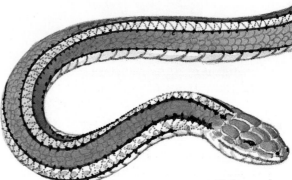

**fleet²** Capable of moving very quickly; swift. The deer is a *fleet* animal.
**fleet** (flēt) *adjective.*

**flex** To bend. If your arm is tired, *flex* it to keep it loose.
**flex** (fleks) *verb,* **flexed, flexing.**

**focus** To adjust one's eyes or a lens in order to make a clear picture or image. The movie on the screen looks fuzzy and needs to be *focused.*
**fo•cus** (fō´kəs) *verb,* **focused, focusing.**

**foreign** Outside a person's own country. Have you ever visited any *foreign* countries?
**for•eign** (fôr´ən) *adjective.*

**formula** A mixture made according to a special recipe. The zookeeper feeds the baby animals a special *formula.*
**for•mu•la** (fôr´myə lə) *noun.*

**fragment** A part that is broken off; small piece. The students found some *fragments* of Native American pottery in the woods.
**frag•ment** (frag´mənt) *noun.*

*fragment*

**freight** Having to do with the carrying of goods by land, air, or water. This *freight* train carries wheat to the city. *Adjective.* —The goods carried in this way; cargo. It took five hours to unload all the *freight* from the train. *Noun.*
**freight** (frāt) *adjective; noun.*

**furious** Very angry. My folks were *furious* when we missed the train by one minute.
**fu•ri•ous** (fyùr´ē əs) *adjective.*

**garter snake** A snake that is green or brown with long yellow stripes on its back. It is harmless to people.
**gar•ter snake** (gär´tər snāk) *noun.*

*garter snake*

**gauze** A very thin cloth that you can see through. It is used in making bandages.
**gauze** (gôz) *noun.*

**gingerly** Very carefully; timidly. The girls walked *gingerly* on the thin ice.
**gin•ger•ly** (jin´jər lē) *adverb.*

**gingko** Another spelling of **ginkgo.** A large tree with fan-shaped leaves. Gingko trees are often planted as ornamental or shade trees.
**ging•ko** (ging´kō) *noun.*

**grater** A kitchen utensil that has a rough surface of sharp, raised edges used to grate vegetables, cheese, spices, and other foods.
**grat•er** (grā´tər) *noun.*

**greaseproof** Not allowing grease, oil, or wax to go through. The clerk wrapped the fish in *greaseproof* paper.
**grease•proof** (grēs´prüf´) *adjective.*

**hammock** A swinging bed that is hung between two trees or poles. It is made from a long piece of canvas or netting.
**ham•mock** (ham´ək) *noun.*

---

**Word History**

The word **hammock** comes from the Spanish word *hamaca*, which in turn came from the language of the Taino, a group of Native Americans of the West Indies.

---

**hayloft** An upper floor in a barn or stable, used for storing hay.
**hay•loft** (hā´lôft´) *noun.*

*hayloft*

**hei yo** (hā´ yō´)

**hemp** A strong, tough fiber made from the stem of a tall plant. It is used to make rope.
**hemp** (hemp) *noun.*

**hinge** A joint on which a door, gate, or lid moves back and forth or up and down. The *hinges* on the old gate squeak when you open or close it. *Noun.* —To depend. The team's chances of winning the championship *hinge* on next week's game. *Verb.*
**hinge** (hinj) *noun; verb,* **hinged, hinging.**

**hoist** To lift or pull up. The sailors *hoisted* the cargo onto the ship's deck with a crane.
**hoist** (hoist) *verb,* **hoisted, hoisting.**

**hover** To stay in the air, flying right above one place. The bees *hovered* over the flowers.
**hov•er** (huv´ər *or* hov´ər) *verb,* **hovered, hovering.**

**humiliate** To make a person feel very ashamed or foolish. My roller-skating ability *humiliated* me this morning, but I can laugh about it now.
**hu•mil•i•ate** (hū mil´ē āt) *verb,* **humiliated, humiliating.**

**illusionary** Caused by or causing a false belief or impression. The picture is *illusionary* because it makes the bottom line look longer.
**il•lu•sion•ar•y** (i lü´zhə ner ē) *adjective.*

---

at; āpe; fär; câre; end; mē; it; īce; pîerce; hot; ōld; sông; fôrk; oil; out; up; ūse; rüle; pùll; tûrn; chin; sing; shop; thin; <u>th</u>is; hw in white; zh in treasure. The symbol ə stands for the unstressed vowel sound in about, taken, pencil, lemon, and circus.

---

**imaginative** Showing the ability to create new images or ideas. The author wrote an *imaginative* story about a genie who had magical powers.
    **i•mag•i•na•tive** (i maj´ə nə tiv) *adjective.*

**indigo** **1.** A deep violet-blue color. **2.** A very dark blue dye that can be obtained from various plants.
    **in•di•go** (in´di gō´) *noun.*

**inflammation** A condition of a part of the body in which there is heat, redness, swelling, and pain. It is usually caused by an infection or injury.
    **in•flam•ma•tion** (in´flə mā´shən) *noun.*

**injustice** Treatment that is not fair or right; unfairness. The class objected to the *injustice* of punishing everyone because one student was noisy.
    **in•jus´tice** (in jus´tis) *noun.*

**inspire** **1.** To bring about. The writer's trip to Mexico *inspired* her latest book. **2.** To stir the mind, feelings, or imagination of. The President's speech *inspired* the country to feel excitement.
    **in•spire** (in spīr´) *verb,* **inspired, inspiring.**

**irritable** Easily made angry or impatient. The child was very *irritable* when he was tired.
    **ir•ri•ta•ble** (ir´i tə bəl) *adjective.*

**jounce** To move or shake up and down roughly. The old wagon *jounced* along the rocky road.
    **jounce** (jouns) *verb,* **jounced, jouncing.**

**jut** To stick out. The lighthouse is on a piece of land that *juts* into the sea.
    **jut** (jut) *verb,* **jutted, jutting.**

*jut*

**kimono** A loose robe that is tied with a sash. Kimonos are worn by both men and women in Japan, usually on holidays or other special occasions.
**ki•mo•no** (ki mō′nə) *noun.*

**kaleidoscope** A tube that contains mirrors and often small pieces of colored glass or other colored objects at one end. When the other end of the tube is held up to the eye and turned, the mirrors reflect a series of changing patterns.
**ka•lei•do•scope** (kə lī′də skōp′) *noun.*

*kimono*

*kaleidoscope*

**kin** A person's whole family; relatives. All of my neighbor's *kin* live in Alabama.
**kin** (kin) *noun.*

---

**Word History**

The word **kaleidoscope** comes from the Greek words *kalos,* meaning "beautiful," *eidos,* meaning "form," and *skopos,* meaning "to look at." Together, these words mean "to look at beautiful forms."

---

at; āpe; fär; câre; end; mē; it; īce; pîerce; hot; ōld; sông; fôrk; oil; out; up; ūse; rüle; pull; tûrn; chin; sing; shop; thin; this; hw in white; zh in treasure. The symbol ə stands for the unstressed vowel sound in about, taken, pencil, lemon, and circus.

# L

**lash¹** To move back and forth quickly. The angry tiger *lashed* its tail.
**lash** (lash) *verb,* **lashed, lashing.**

**lash²** To tie with a rope. The shipwrecked sailors *lashed* some boards together to make a raft.
**lash** (lash) *verb,* **lashed, lashing.**

*lash²*

**latch** To fasten or close something, usually with a small bar of metal or wood. We were in a hurry and forgot to *latch* the back door.
**latch** (lach) *verb,* **latched, latching.**

**Little Soo** (lit´əl sü)

**Lon Po Po** (lon pô pô *or* lōng bô bô)

# M

**machete** A broad, heavy knife used as a tool and weapon.
**ma•chet•e** (mə shet´ē *or* mə chet´ē) *noun.*

**magnify** To make something look bigger than it really is. The microscope *magnified* the cells one hundred times.
**mag•ni•fy** (mag´nə fī´) *verb,* **magnified, magnifying.**

**masterpiece** **1.** Something that is done with great skill. The house she built was a *masterpiece.* **2.** A person's greatest achievement or finest work. This painting is considered the artist's *masterpiece.*
**mas•ter•piece** (mas´tər pēs´) *noun.*

**material** Cloth made from cotton, wool, silk, linen, or other fibers.
**ma•te•ri•al** (mə tîr´ē əl) *noun.*

*material*

**maternity** Having to do with the care of newborn babies and women during and after the birth of a baby. The mother and her new baby rested in the *maternity* ward of the hospital.
**ma•ter•ni•ty** (mə tûr´ni tē) *adjective.*

**mend** **1.** To heal; improve. The doctor said that my sprained ankle has *mended* nicely. **2.** To put in good condition again; fix or repair. I *mended* the broken cup using glue.
   **mend** (mend) *verb,* **mended, mending.**

**mica** Any of a group of minerals that look like transparent or cloudy glass and that can be separated into thin sheets.
   **mi•ca** (mī´ kə) *noun.*

*mica*

**mijito** Spanish for "little one."
   **mi•ji•to** (mē hē´tō) *noun.*

**mischievous** Playful. That *mischievous* child hid my slippers again.
   **mis•chie•vous** (mis´chə vəs) *adjective.*

**misunderstanding** **1.** The act of not understanding correctly. *Misunderstandings* sometimes lead to mistakes. **2.** A quarrel or argument between people. The two friends settled their *misunderstandings* by discussing them.
   **mis•un•der•stand•ing** (mis´un dər stan´ding) *noun.*

**morsel** A small bite of food or piece of something. The birds ate every *morsel* of bread we put out for them.
   **mor•sel** (môr´səl) *noun.*

**moss** A small green plant that grows in groups to form a soft, thick mat on the ground, on rocks, or on trees. Mosses grow in shady places where it is damp.
   **moss** (môs) *noun.*

*moss*

at; āpe; fär; câre; end; mē; it; īce; pîerce; hot; ōld; sông; fôrk; oil; out; up; ūse; rüle; pu̇ll; tûrn; chin; sing; shop; thin; **th**is; hw in **wh**ite; zh in treasure. The symbol ə stands for the unstressed vowel sound in about, taken, pencil, lemon, and circus.

# N

**namesake** A person named after or having the same name as another. Charlie is his father's *namesake*. His father is named Charlie, too.
    **name•sake** (nām′sāk′) *noun*.

**niño** Spanish for "little boy."
    **ni•ño** (nēn′yō) *noun*.

# O

**oblong** Having a shape that is longer than it is wide. The necktie was in an *oblong* box.
    **ob•long** (ob′ lông′) *adjective*.

**oilcloth** A waterproof fabric made by coating cloth with oil or a similar substance. It is used for tablecloths, shelf lining, cushion covers, and other things.
    **oil•cloth** (oil′ klôth′) *noun*.

**outfox** To outwit; outsmart. We *outfoxed* the other team by trying two new strategies we had practiced.
    **out•fox** (out′foks′) *verb*, **outfoxed, outfoxing.**

**outgrow** To grow too big for something. A baby *outgrows* her clothes within weeks.
    **out•grow** (out′grō′) *verb*, **outgrew, outgrown, outgrowing.**

**overjoyed** Very happy. We were *overjoyed* when we heard that our school's team had won the championship.
    **o•ver•joyed** (ō′vər joid′) *adjective*.

*overjoyed*

**overwhelming** Having great power or intensity; overpowering. The force of the tornado was *overwhelming*.
    **o•ver•whelm•ing** (ō′vər hwel′ming or ō′vər wel′ming) *adjective*.

# P

**page¹** One side of a sheet of paper in a book, newspaper, or magazine. Find the exact *page* in the book where the story begins.
    **page** (pāj) *noun.*

**page²** To try to find someone by calling out his or her name. They *paged* the pilot over the loudspeaker in the airport.
    **page** (pāj) *verb,* **paged, paging.**

**Paotze** (pou´dzə)

**particle** A very small bit or piece of something. A *particle* of dirt flew into my eye.
    **par•ti•cle** (pär´ti kəl) *noun.*

**pavilion** A building or other structure that is used for a show or exhibit, or for recreation. A pavilion often has open sides. The dance was held at a *pavilion* in the park.
    **pa•vil•ion** (pə vil´yən) *noun.*

**peak** The pointed top of a high mountain. We could see the snowy *peak* in the distance. ▲ Another word that sounds like this is **peek.**
    **peak** (pēk) *noun.*

**periscope** An instrument that looks like a telescope and sticks out from the top of a submarine. It is used to see ships, land, or other things above the surface of the water.
    **per•i•scope** (per´ə skōp´) *noun.*

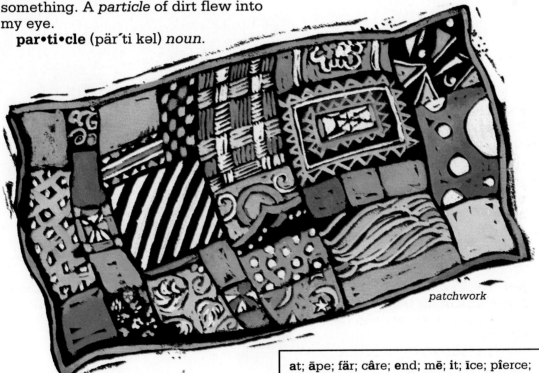

*patchwork*

**patchwork** Made or covered with pieces of cloth sewn together. She made a *patchwork* pillow.
    **patch•work** (pach´wûrk´) *adjective.*

at; āpe; fär; câre; end; mē; it; īce; pîerce; hot; ōld; sông; fôrk; oil; out; up; ūse; rüle; pùll; tûrn; chin; sing; shop; thin; <u>th</u>is; hw in white; zh in treasure. The symbol ə stands for the unstressed vowel sound in about, taken, pencil, lemon, and circus.

**permeate** To pass through the holes, pores, or openings of. Water will not *permeate* this fabric.
  **per•me•ate** (pûr´mē āt´) *verb,* **permeated, permeating.**

**philosophy** A person's principles and beliefs. My parents' *philosophy* is to be kind to others.
  **phi•los•o•phy** (fə los´ə fē) *noun, plural* **philosophies.**

**pitch-black** Extremely black.
  **pitch-black** (pich´ blak´) *adjective.*

**pitiful** Causing sorrow and sympathy. The lost puppy looked so *pitiful* that we took it home and kept it as a pet.
  **pit•i•ful** (pit´i fəl) *adjective.*

**plead** To make a sincere request; beg. I *pleaded* with my friend not to swim near the rocks.
  **plead** (plēd) *verb,* **pleaded, pleading.**

**plump** Full and round; nicely fat. That healthy baby has *plump*, rosy cheeks.
  **plump** (plump) *adjective.*

**plunge** 1. To dive or fall suddenly. The swimmer *plunged* into the pool. 2. To put in suddenly. I *plunged* my hand into the water to try to catch the fish.
  **plunge** (plunj) *verb,* **plunged, plunging.**

*plunge*

**predicament** An unpleasant or difficult situation; fix. Look at the *predicament* you're in because you accepted two invitations for the same day!
pre•dic•a•ment (pri dik´ə mənt) *noun.*

**preparation** Something put together for a purpose. That medicine is a *preparation* to help stop coughing.
prep•a•ra•tion (prep´ə rā´shən) *noun.*

**prescription** An order written by a doctor to a pharmacist for medicine. The doctor gave me a *prescription* for cough medicine.
pre•scrip•tion (pri skrip´shən) *noun.*

*prescription*

**proceed** To begin some action. Héctor cleared his throat and *proceeded* to speak.
pro•ceed (prə sēd´) *verb,* proceeded, proceeding.

---

**Word History**

The word **proceed** comes from *pro-*, a Latin word beginning that means "forward," and the Latin word *cedere*, meaning "to go."

---

**promptly** Quickly or on time. The meal in the restaurant was served *promptly.*
prompt•ly (prompt´ lē) *adverb.*

**prong** One of the pointed ends of an antler or of a fork or other tool.
prong (prông *or* prong) *noun.*

*prong*

**put-up** Preserved, as in canned or pickled foods. The woman canned the peaches and later placed the jars of *put-up* fruit on the shelf.
put-up (pu̇t´up´) *adjective.*

---

at; āpe; fär; câre; end; mē; it; īce; pîerce; hot; ōld; sông; fôrk; oil; out; up; ūse; rüle; pu̇ll; tûrn; chin; sing; shop; thin; **this**; hw in white; zh in treasure. The symbol ə stands for the unstressed vowel sound in about, taken, pencil, lemon, and circus.

---

# Q

**quail** A bird that has a plump body and brown or gray feathers often dotted with white. This bird is also called a **partridge.**
**quail** (kwāl) *noun.*

*quail*

**quench** To put an end to by satisfying. I will *quench* my thirst with a long drink of water.
**quench** (kwench) *verb,* **quenched, quenching.**

**quilt** A bed covering made of two pieces of cloth that are stuffed with soft material. The two pieces of cloth are held together by lines of stitching that are sewn all over the surface of the cloth. *Noun.* —To stitch together with a soft lining. *Verb.*
**quilt** (kwilt) *noun; verb,* **quilted, quilting.**

**quiver** To shake slightly; shiver. The leaves began to *quiver* in the breeze.
**quiv•er** (kwiv´ər) *verb,* **quivered, quivering.**

# R

**radiant** Shining brightly; beaming. We shielded our eyes from the *radiant* summer sun. The child's face was *radiant* from the excitement of winning.
**ra•di•ant** (rā´dē ənt) *adjective.*

**rap** A style of popular music in which rhyming lyrics are spoken in a rapid way, set to a simple, repetitive beat.
**rap** (rap) *noun.*

**reflect** To give back an image of something. The pond *reflects* my image.
**re•flect** (ri flekt´) *verb,* **reflected, reflecting.**

**reflection** An image given back by a surface such as a mirror or a pond. I looked at my *reflection* in the store window.
**re•flec•tion** (ri flek´shən) *noun.*

*reflection*

**refreshing** Restoring strength; making fresh again. The cold drink was very *refreshing* after the long hike.
**re•fresh•ing** (ri fresh´ing) *adjective.*

*remains*

**remains** Something that is left. The explorers found the *remains* of an ancient city.
> **re•mains** (ri mānz´) *plural noun.*

**remarkable** Worthy of being noticed; not ordinary; unusual. Your science project is *remarkable*.
> **re•mark•a•ble** (ri mär´kə bəl) *adjective.*

**rhythm** A regular or orderly repeating of sounds or movements. We marched to the *rhythm* of a steady drumbeat.
> **rhythm** (ri<u>th</u>´əm) *noun.*

**risk** To take a chance of loss or harm. My parents *risked* losing money when they bought a store.
> **risk** (risk) *verb,* **risked, risking.**

**rivalry** Competition; trying to be as good as or better than another person. There was great *rivalry* between the two girls in basketball.
> **ri•val•ry** (rī´vəl rē) *noun, plural* **rivalries.**

**route** A road or other course used for traveling. We drove along the ocean *route* to the beach. ▲ Another word that sounds like this is **root.**
> **route** (rüt *or* rout) *noun.*

---

at; āpe; fär; câre; **e**nd; mē; **i**t; īce; pîerce; hot; ōld; sông; fôrk; **oi**l; **ou**t; **u**p; ūse; rüle; p**u**ll; tûrn; **ch**in; si**ng**; **sh**op; **th**in; <u>th</u>is; **hw** in **wh**ite; **zh** in trea**s**ure. The symbol ə stands for the unstressed vowel sound in **a**bout, tak**e**n, penc**i**l, lem**o**n, and circ**u**s.

*rubbish*

**rubbish** Useless waste material;
trash. Put all the *rubbish* in a pile by
the back door.
**rub•bish** (rub´ish) *noun.*

**ruckus** A loud noise or commotion;
an uproar. The noisy students made
quite a *ruckus* in the playground.
**ruck•us** (ruk´əs) *noun.*

# S

**salamander** An animal that looks
like a small lizard. Salamanders are
amphibians and are related to frogs
and toads. They live in or near fresh
water.
**sal•a•man•der** (sal´ə man´dər)
*noun.*

**salary** A fixed amount of money that
is paid to someone for work done. It
is paid at regular times. That job
pays a good *salary.*
**sal•a•ry** (sal´ə rē) *noun, plural*
**salaries.**

**sanitation** The protection of people's
health by keeping living conditions
clean. Sanitation includes getting rid
of garbage and keeping drinking
water clean.
**san•i•ta•tion** (san´i tā´shən) *noun.*

**scale¹** A device used to find out how
heavy something is. It works by
balancing the thing to be weighed
against another weight or against
the force of a spring.
**scale** (skāl) *noun.*

**scale²** One of the thin, flat plates
that cover the bodies of fish, lizards,
crocodiles, and other reptiles.
**scale** (skāl) *noun.*

*scale²*

*sibling*

**scout** One who is sent out to find and bring back information. The *scout* brought back word that the enemy was camped nearby.
    **scout** (skout) *noun.*

**seize** **1.** To take hold of; grab. The dog *seized* the bone. **2.** To get control of; capture. The soldiers were ordered to *seize* the fort.
    **seize** (sēz) *verb,* **seized, seizing.**

**senseless** Unconscious. The blow knocked me *senseless.*
    **sense•less** (sens´ lis) *adjective.*

**shabby** **1.** Mean or unfair. It's cruel and *shabby* to make fun of other people. **2.** Worn out and faded. This old shirt looks *shabby.*
    **shab•by** (shab´ē) *adjective.*

**Shang** (shang *or* shông)

**shuffleboard** A game played by pushing disks with a special stick on a smooth, level surface.
    **shuf•fle•board** (shuf´əl bôrd´) *noun.*

**sibling** A brother or sister. Kim is Chan's *sibling.*
    **sib•ling** (sib´ ling) *noun.*

**slope** To lie or cause to lie at an angle between flat and upright. The road *slopes* toward the river.
    **slope** (slōp) *verb,* **sloped, sloping.**

**smokehouse** A building where meat or fish is treated with smoke to preserve and flavor it.
    **smoke•house** (smōk´ hous´) *noun.*

**socket** An opening into which something fits. She screwed the light bulb into the *socket.*
    **sock•et** (sok´it) *noun.*

---

at; āpe; fär; câre; end; mē; it; īce; pîerce; hot; ōld; sông; fôrk; oil; out; up; ūse; rüle; pùll; tûrn; chin; sing; shop; thin; this; hw in white; zh in treasure. The symbol ə stands for the unstressed vowel sound in about, taken, pencil, lemon, and circus.

**squirm** To turn or twist the body; wriggle. The children were bored and *squirmed* in their seats.
   **squirm** (skwûrm) *verb,* **squirmed, squirming.**

**station** To place in a particular position. We *stationed* ourselves by the door.
   **sta•tion** (stā´shən) *verb,* **stationed, stationing.**

**steep²** To soak in water or another liquid. I *steeped* the peppermint leaves in hot water to make tea.
   **steep** (stēp) *verb,* **steeped, steeping.**

**stethoscope** An instrument used by doctors and nurses to listen to heartbeats and other sounds in the body.
   **steth•o•scope** (steth´ə skōp´) *noun.*

*stethoscope*

**steamer trunk** A large rectangular box with a lid used for carrying and storing things on a steamship.
   **steam•er trunk** (stē´mər trungk) *noun.*

**steep¹** Having a very sharp slope. It was difficult to ride our bicycles up the *steep* hill.
   **steep** (stēp) *adjective.*

**stun** 1. To shock. We were *stunned* by the news. 2. To make unconscious. The robin was *stunned* when it flew into the window.
   **stun** (stun) *verb,* **stunned, stunning.**

**suitable** Right; proper. The soil in our backyard is *suitable* for growing tomatoes.
   **suit•a•ble** (sü´tə bəl) *adjective.*

*sukiyaki*

**sukiyaki** A Japanese dish made of thin strips of meat and vegetables, cooked quickly, usually at the dining table.

    **su•ki•ya•ki** (sü′kē yä′ kē *or* skē yä′ kē) *noun.*

**surface** The upper or outer part of a thing. The *surface* of the stone is rough.

    **sur•face** (sûr′fis) *noun.*

**surround** To be on all sides of; form a circle around. A fence *surrounds* our yard.

    **sur•round** (sə round′) *verb,* **surrounded, surrounding.**

**suspend** To attach so as to hang down. The swing was *suspended* from a tree branch.

    **sus•pend** (sə spend′) *verb,* **suspended, suspending.**

**suspicion** A thought that something is possible or true. My *suspicion* that the apple was rotten turned out to be correct.

    **sus•pi•cion** (sə spish′ən) *noun.*

**swerve** To turn aside suddenly. The driver *swerved* to avoid hitting a dog.

    **swerve** (swûrv) *verb,* **swerved, swerving.**

**sympathy** The ability to feel and understand the sorrow or troubles of others. I had *sympathy* for the hurt dog.

    **sym•pa•thy** (sim′pə thē) *noun.*

**Tang** (tang *or* tông)

**tangram** A Chinese puzzle made by cutting a square into seven geometric pieces, called *tans.* All seven pieces must be used to make a picture.

    **tan•gram** (tang′grəm) *noun.*

---

**Word History**

    The word **tangram** may come from the Chinese word *t'ang,* meaning "Chinese," and the English word ending *-gram,* which comes from the Greek word *gramma,* meaning "drawing" or "writing."

---

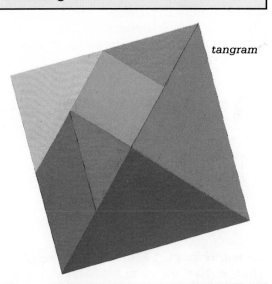

*tangram*

---

at; āpe; fär; câre; **e**nd; mē; it; īce; pîerce; hot; ōld; sông; fôrk; oil; out; up; ūse; rüle; pu̇ll; tûrn; **ch**in; si**ng**; **sh**op; **th**in; **th̲**is; **hw** in **wh**ite; **zh** in trea**s**ure. The symbol **ə** stands for the unstressed vowel sound in **a**bout, tak**e**n, penc**i**l, lem**o**n, and circ**u**s.

**Tao** (tou *or* dou)

**tar** A dark, sticky substance that is made from coal or wood. Tar is used to pave roads and to waterproof roofs and sheds.
tar (tär) *noun.*

**tend** To take care of; look after. Our neighbor *tended* our plants while we were away on vacation.
tend (tend) *verb,* **tended, tending.**

**texture** The look and feel of something. Sandpaper and brick have rough *textures.*
tex•ture (teks´chər) *noun.*

**ticking** A strong fabric made of closely woven cotton or linen. Ticking is often used to make covers for mattresses and pillows.
tick•ing (tik´ing) *noun.*

**tilt** To raise one end or side of; put at an angle; tip. He *tilted* his chair back and fell over.
tilt (tilt) *verb,* **tilted, tilting.**

**timid** Easily frightened; lacking courage or boldness; shy. The *timid* child was afraid to speak up in class.
tim•id (tim´id) *adjective.*

**tofu** A soft, white food made from mashed soybeans and formed into a cake. Tofu is used especially in Asian and vegetarian cooking. Tofu is also called **bean curd.**
to•fu (tō´fü) *noun.*

**tragic** Very sad or dreadful. The plane crash was a *tragic* accident.
trag•ic (traj´ik) *adjective.*

**transform** To change the way a person or thing looks. The caterpillar *transformed* into a butterfly.
trans•form (trans fôrm´) *verb,* **transformed, transforming.**

**treatment** The care or medicine used to help cure a sick or injured person. Rest was the recommended *treatment.*
treat•ment (trēt´mənt) *noun.*

**tremble** To shake with cold, fear, weakness, or anger. The wet kitten *trembled.*
trem•ble (trem´ bəl) *verb,* **trembled, trembling.**

**trumpeter** A person who gives signals by blowing a trumpet.
trum•pet•er (trum´pi tər) *noun.*

*trumpeter*

**twilight** The time just after sunset or just before sunrise when there is a soft, hazy light.
    **twi•light** (twī′līt′) *noun.*

**utensil** An object or tool that is useful or necessary in doing or making something. I keep all my cooking *utensils* in a drawer.
    **u•ten•sil** (ū ten′səl) *noun.*

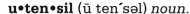
utensil

# U

**unaware** Not knowing or realizing; not aware. We were *unaware* that the road ahead was closed.
    **un•a•ware** (un′ə wâr′) *adjective.*

**unbearably** In a way, or to such an extent, that one cannot bear or endure it. The icy water of the lake was *unbearably* cold.
    **un•bear•a•bly** (un bâr′ə blē′) *adverb.*

**unexpected** Coming or happening without warning; not expected. The bus was late because of an *unexpected* traffic jam.
    **un•ex•pect•ed** (un′ek spek′tid) *adjective.*

**unique** Not having an equal; being the only one of its kind. Being the first person to set foot on the moon was a *unique* achievement.
    **u•nique** (ū nēk′) *adjective.*

**unnatural** Going against or different from what is usual or normal in nature; not natural. The cat grew to an *unnatural* size.
    **un•nat•u•ral** (un nach′ər əl) *adjective.*

# V

**vanish** To go out of sight or existence; disappear. The airplane *vanished* above the clouds.
    **van•ish** (van′ish) *verb,* **vanished, vanishing.**

**veer** To change direction or course; shift; turn. At the bottom of the hill the road *veers* sharply to the left.
    **veer** (vîr) *verb,* **veered, veering.**

---

at; āpe; fär; câre; end; mē; it; īce; pîerce; hot; ōld; sông; fôrk; oil; out; up; ūse; rüle; pull; tûrn; chin; sing; shop; thin; this; hw in white; zh in treasure. The symbol ə stands for the unstressed vowel sound in about, taken, pencil, lemon, and circus.

---

**vertical** Straight up and down; upright. The walls of a building are in a *vertical* position.
**ver•ti•cal** (vûr´ti kəl) *adjective.*

**violently** In a way that is caused by or shows strong physiçal force.
**vi•o•lent•ly** (vī´ə lənt lē) *adverb.*

# W

**waltz** **1.** A whirling, gliding dance that is performed by a couple. **2.** The music for this dance.
**waltz** (wôlts) *noun.*

**ward** A large room or section of a hospital. A number of patients are taken care of in a ward.
**ward** (wôrd) *noun.*

**wedge** Something forming a shape that is wide at one end and narrow at the other. We served a *wedge* of cheese with crackers.
**wedge** (wej) *noun.*

**Westerner** A person who is living in the western part of a country or of the world. People living in the United States are *Westerners* to people living in Japan. People in Colorado are *Westerners* to people in Vermont.
**West•ern•er** (wes´tər nər) *noun.*

**whimsical** Unusual or odd in a way that shows imagination. The artist's *whimsical* drawings of animals dressed like people delighted the children.
**whim•si•cal** (hwim´zi kəl *or* wim´zi kəl) *adjective.*

**whirlpool** A current of water that moves quickly in a circle.
**whirl•pool** (hwûrl´pül´ *or* wûrl´pül´) *noun.*

**winch** A machine for lifting or pulling things. A winch is made up of a large spool or pulley with a rope or chain around it. Ships' anchors are hoisted on a winch.
**winch** (winch) *noun.*

**windrow** A long row of hay, straw, or grain raked together to dry before being collected.
**wind•row** (wind´rō) *noun.*

*windrow*

**woozy** Dizzy; dazed. The man felt *woozy* after he bumped his head.
**wooz•y** (wü´zē *or* wùz´ē) *adjective.*

**Wu Ling** (wü ling)

# Y

**yearling** One year old. The boy takes care of the *yearling* calf.
**year•ling** (yîr´ ling) *adjective.*

**Yokohama** A port city in east-central Japan.
**Yo•ko•ha•ma** (yō´kə hä´mə) *noun.*